Conference Proceedings of the Society for Experimental Mechanics Series

Series Editor

Kristin B. Zimmerman
Society for Experimental Mechanics, Inc.,
Bethel, USA

The Conference Proceedings of the Society for Experimental Mechanics Series presents early findings and case studies from a wide range of fundamental and applied work across the broad range of fields that comprise Experimental Mechanics. Series volumes follow the principle tracks or focus topics featured in each of the Society's two annual conferences: IMAC, A Conference and Exposition on Structural Dynamics, and the Society's Annual Conference & Exposition and will address critical areas of interest to researchers and design engineers working in all areas of Structural Dynamics, Solid Mechanics and Materials Research.

Emily Retzlaff · Piyush Thakre · Marco Rossi · Sharlotte Kramer
Editors

Mechanics of Additive & Advanced Manufacturing, Inverse Methods and Machine Learning, Vol. 5

Proceedings of the 2025 Annual Conference
on Experimental and Applied Mechanics

River Publishers

Published, sold and distributed by:

River Publishers
Broagervej 10
9260 Gistrup
Denmark

www.riverpublishers.com

ISBN 97887-438-0831-2 (Hardback)

ISBN 97887-438-0836-7 (eBook)

https://doi.org/10.13052/97887-438-0831-2

Conference Proceedings of the Society for Experimental Mechanics

An imprint of River Publishers

Preface

Mechanics of Additive and Advanced Manufacturing, Inverse Methods and Machine Learning represents one of five volumes of technical papers presented at the 2025 SEM Annual Conference & Exposition on Experimental and Applied Mechanics organized by the Society for Experimental Mechanics and held in Milwaukee, WI, June 2-5, 2025. The complete Proceedings also includes volumes on: *Dynamic Behavior of Materials; Advancement of Optical Methods & Digital Image Correlation in Experimental Mechanics; and Mechanics of Biological Systems and Materials and the Mechanics of Composite, Hybrid & Multifunctional Materials; and Fracture, Fatigue, Failure, Damage Evolution and Thermomechanics & Infrared Imaging.*

Mechanics of Additive and Advanced Manufacturing is an emerging area due to the unprecedented design and manufacturing possibilities offered by new and evolving advanced manufacturing processes and the rich mechanics issues that emerge. Technical interest within the Society spans several other SEM Technical Divisions such as: Composites, Hybrids and Multifunctional Materials, Dynamic Behavior of Materials, Fracture and Fatigue, Residual Stress, Time-dependent Materials, and the Research Committee.

The topic of mechanics of additive and advanced manufacturing included in this volume covers design, optimization, experiments, computations, and materials for advanced manufacturing processes (3D printing, micro- and nano-manufacturing, powder bed fusion, directed energy deposition, etc.) with particular focus on mechanics aspects (e.g. mechanical properties, residual stress, deformation, failure, rate-dependent mechanical behavior, etc.).

The topic of Inverse Methods and Machine Learning included in this volume covers the Virtual Fields Method, inverse methods for plasticity, identification for anisotropic and heterogeneous materials, optimal experimental design for inverse methods, and machine learning for mechanics with an emphasis on inverse methods.

Editors:
Emily Retzlaff – *United States Naval Academy, Annapolis, MD, USA*; Piyush Thakre, *Dow Inc., TX, USA*; Marco Rossi, *Universita Politecnica Delle Marche, Italy*; Sharlotte Kramer, *Sandia National Laboratories, NM, USA.*

Contents

Chapter 1
Effect of Coatings and Additives on the Water Absorption and Mechanical Characteristics of Additive Manufactured Nylon Polymers

James LeBlanc, Irine Chenwi, Julianna Martinez, Olivia Dube, Dillon Fontaine, Eric Warner, Tyler Chu, Arun Shukla, and Lewis Shattuck

Abstract The use of baseline material data taken in controlled laboratory conditions on dry, unaged specimens is largely insufficient for the design of critical structures to be deployed in deep-water, wetted applications. Recent studies have shown that Nylon based materials absorb a substantial amount of water when exposed to marine environments. This effort conducted an experimental investigation of the effectiveness of surface coatings and material additives on the reduction of water absorption into nylon based AM polymers and the corresponding effects on the mechanical properties of the materials. The study is divided into two unique parts: (1) effects of post print surface coatings on 3D printed specimens, and (2) effects of nanoclay additives on nylon base material. The study's findings highlight that the use of surface coatings and nanoclay additives can reduce the amount of salt water absorbed by the respective materials. However, the coatings and nanoclays also have a degrading effect on the mechanical properties of the materials themselves, even in the absence of salt water exposure. Therefore, significant consideration must be given to material selection when choosing surface coatings and material additives. Similarly, the use of nanoclay additives are shown to change the material behavior from highly ductile to highly brittle. These changes can potentially cause premature failures when utilized with AM polymers without detailed material characterization data obtained before and after salt water exposure.

Keywords Additive Manufacturing · Mechanical characterization · Water absorption · Material Additives · Surface Coatings

Introduction

Additive Manufacturing (AM) is one of the largest growing areas of novel manufacturing approaches, with applications ranging from home hobbyists up to full scale commercial production of parts. The technology lends itself to ready access to parts on demand, ease of manufacture for complex designs not otherwise possible, shorter design to manufacturing cycle times (rapid prototyping), lightweight designs, and cost savings. These manufacturing techniques provide the ability to achieve part geometries not possible with "subtractive" manufacturing methods (e.g. CNC milling), and eliminate the need for complex and expensive tooling/molds when small part quantities are needed, for example ad-hoc spare parts in an on-demand setting. Despite these advantages, there are also associated disadvantages with these technologies such as potential part variability based on print parameters, print post-processing, and increased part porosity.

The effects of moisture and water absorption on the performance of additively printed materials has become a recent topic of research interests. Research findings have shown moisture and water absorption can result in decreases in modulus,

James LeBlanc · Irine Chenwi · Julianna Martinez · Olivia Dube · Dillon Fontaine · Eric Warner · Lewis Shattuck
Naval Undersea Warfare Center (Division Newport), Newport, RI 02841
e-mail: james.m.leblanc.civ@us.navy.mil; irine.n.chenwi.civ@us.navy.mil; julianna.a.martinez3.civ@us.navy.mil; olivia.m.dube.civ@us.navy.mil; dillon.t.fontaine.civ@us.navy.mil; eric.a.warner8.civ@us.navy.mil; lewis.b.shattuck.civ@us.navy.mil

Tyler Chu · Arun Shukla
Dynamic Photo Mechanics Laboratory, Department of Mechanical, Industrial and Systems Engineering, University of Rhode Island, Kingston, RI 02881
e-mail: tylerchu@uri.edu; shuklaa@uri.edu

Emily Retzlaff et al. (eds.), *Mechanics of Additive & Advanced Manufacturing, Inverse Methods and Machine Learning, Vol. 5*, Conference Proceedings of the Society for Experimental Mechanics Series, https://doi.org/10.13052/9788743808312-1

ultimate tensile strength, decreased energy release rate (GIC), and stress intensity factor (KIC). These studies have investigated common AM polymers such as ABS, PLA, and PETG. In addition to the specific materials themselves, the effect of layer thickness and associated print parameters can affect water absorption levels and material swelling. Furthermore, the effectiveness of post print surface treatments and coatings to reduce water absorption for FDM printed materials have been the subject of recent publications. Recently, the effects of salt water exposure have been investigated and highlighted the base material composition is a key contributor to the level of material degradation due to saline fluid exposure.

Materials

There are several distinct materials utilized in the study, which are categorized into baseline filaments, filament additives, and post print coatings. The Markforged Onyx material is utilized to manufacture mechanical specimens that were subsequently coated with one of two surface treatments. The Nylon filament was used as a base material to which the nanoclay additive was added to through a secondary filament extrusion process. Markforged Onyx is a nylon-based material, which contains micro carbon fibers, with a nominal material density of 1.2 g/cm^3. The first post-print surface treatment applied to the Markforged Onyx specimens was an epoxy hardpot coating, Henkel Loctite Stycast 2651 Epoxy Encapsulant which was mixed with Henkel Loctite Catalyst 9. The second post-print surface treatment applied to the Markforged Onyx specimens was an epoxy based paint system, Sherwin Williams E2A933 Epoxy Primer and Sherwin Williams Genesis GC 3.5 Automotive Top Coat. Markforged Nylon is a pure nylon-based material with a nominal material density of 1.1 g/cm^3. The nanoclay powder that was used as an additive for the Markforged Nylon was Sigma-Aldrich Montmorillonite Clay (MMT) with surface modification, particle size of <= 20 microns, and a density of 200-500 kg/m^3. The nylon material was pelletized and subsequently combined with the nanoclay additives at weight percentages of 2% and 5%. Two extrusion cycles were carried out for each nylon composite to ensure that the nanoclay was sufficiently dispersed in the nylon.

Water Absorption and Mechanical Characterization

The water immersion of the epoxy hardpot and painted Markforged Onyx specimens was carried out in a novel test facility specifically designed for high-pressure water immersion experiments. The material specimens were placed in a 3.5% NaCl solution, pressurized to 5000 psi, and were left untouched for 60 days. The water immersion study for the nylon specimens with nanoclay additives was performed at ambient pressure and at room temperature. Both the neat nylon and nylon composites were immersed in a 3.5% NaCl solution for 30 days. The coated Markforged Onyx specimens were characterized for the following properties before and after the 60-day immersion: Tension, Compression and Flexure per ASTM standards. The Nylon with nanoclay additives underwent the following characterization: thermogravimetric analysis (TGA), Differential Scanning Calorimetry (DSC), Dynamic Mechanical Analysis (DMA), and Tension.

Results

This effort conducted an experimental investigation of the effectiveness of surface coatings and material additives on the reduction of water absorption into nylon based AM polymers and the corresponding effects on the mechanical properties of the materials. The study is divided into two unique parts: (1) effects of post print surface coatings on 3D printed specimens, and (2) effects of nanoclay additives on nylon base material. The study's findings highlight that the use of surface coatings and nanoclay additives can reduce the amount of salt water absorbed by the respective materials. The surface coatings that were applied to the AM printed specimens were found to be effective in reducing both the rate of water absorption and the overall mass change due to water absorption from 6% to 3%. The incorporation of nanoclay additive into the baseline nylon material was shown to reduce the amount of mass absorbed during salt water immersion from 1.7% to 1.6%. The thermogravimetric analysis was performed to quantify the thermal decomposition of the baseline nylon and nanoclay modified nylon. The baseline nylon experienced the onset of decomposition at a temperature of 416 °C and the nanoclay modified material showed the onset of decomposition at 406 °C and 397 °C for the 2% and 5% material respectively. DSC quantified the changes in the thermal properties of the nylon and modified nylon materials. The quantities of interest included glass transition temperature (Tg) and melting temperature (Tm). The glass transition temperature for the pure nylon, 2% nanoclay, and 5% nanoclay materials were 45°C, 44°C and 43 °C, respectively. The melting temperatures were found to be 200 °C for the pure nylon, 203 °C and 204 °C for the 2% and 5% nanoclay materials. Therefore, the inclusion of the nanoclays into the nylon lower the T_g and increase the T_m temperatures. The tension, compression, and flexure testing of the surface coated material indicate that both the coatings and salt water exposure affect the mechanical behavior of the Markforged Onyx material. When coated with both the epoxy hardpot and paint there is a reduction in modulus and strength as compared to the dry uncoated material. For each coating configuration there is a further drop in both stiffness and tensile strength after 60-day salt water exposure. The incorporation of the nanoclay additive into the pure nylon baseline material had two adverse effects on the tensile behavior of the material. The first is that the tensile strength of the nylon was reduced by the nanoclays, with the 2% nanoclay specimens having a lower strength than the 5% specimens. More significantly, the inclusion of the nanoclays changed the behavior of the nylon from a highly ductile material to one of high brittleness. The tensile strain at failure was reduced from above 100% for the nylon itself to 2% when nanoclay was incorporated. DMA results show that adding nanoclay increases the stresses and storage and loss moduli of the composite materials. The presence of the clay also reduced the overall loss in stiffness associated to water ingression. There was a remarkable increase in stiffness when the wet samples were tested at -2°C indicating that the water had changed to solid. The nanoclays led to an overall brittleness in the nylon composites for both dry and wet samples.

Acknowledgments The research presented in this study has been generously supported through the Internal Investment Program at Naval Undersea Warfare Center (NUWC) Division Newport. The authors greatly acknowledge the assistance of Jennifer M. Szarkowicz (NUWC Division Newport) in producing the 3D-printed samples for this study.

Chapter 2
Electrically Aligned Epoxy-Based Nanocomposites: Processing and Characterization

Rahman Julkarnyne M. Habibur and Gururaja Suhasini

Abstract This study examines the electric-field alignment of amine-functionalized multi-walled carbon nanotubes (MWCNTs) within an epoxy matrix, aiming to enhance their mechanical, electrical, and thermal performance. Amine-functionalized MWCNTs were dispersed within the epoxy resin using high-shear mixing to achieve a homogenous nanocomposite. 0.1, 0.2, 0.3 wt% of nanomaterials are used to prepare the samples. A key feature of the research involved the application of an external AC electric field before curing to align MWCNTs in the desired orientation. The voltage and the distance of electrodes were varied to examine the effect of the AC electric field on the alignment time. Response surface methodology (RSM), along with the central composite design (CCD), has been used to analyze the influence of those process parameters. Analysis of variance (ANOVA) was performed to identify the significant parameters. A voltage of 1000V and a distance of 50 mm between the electrodes was the optimal solution to minimize the alignment time while aligning MWCNTs in the epoxy matrix.

Keywords Nanocomposite · Electric field alignment · ANOVA · RSM · Optimization

Introduction

Polymer matrix composites (PMCs) are the combinations of different organic polymers with reinforced fibers. Manufacturers can produce PMCs from polymers such as thermoplastics and thermosets. Because of their excellent mechanical properties, thermal stability, and chemical resistance, people widely employ epoxy resins—the most commonly used thermoset—in the aerospace, automotive, and electronics industries [1]. Nanofillers, such as carbon nanotubes, can further enhance the performance of epoxy resins. The efficacy of these epoxy-nanocomposites hinges on various factors such as the dispersion quality [2], [3], weight fraction [2], and alignment [4], [5], [6], [7] of nanofillers in the epoxy matrix.

Alignment is generally done by applying external forces such as an electric field [8], magnetic means [6], high-shear mixing, etc. Electric field-assisted alignment has emerged as a versatile technique for orienting conductive MWCNTs, achievable via alternating (AC) or direct (DC) potential fields. Pothnis et al. [9] used the non-uniform AC electric field to align the CNTs, and Khan et al. [10] and Oliva et al. [11] used the DC electric field to align the CNTs in the matrix. The alignment time mostly depends on the rotation and migration of the MWCNTs in the epoxy matrix [12]. Viscosity plays a major role in the alignment as the lower viscosity facilitates the alignment [13]. Factors such as voltage and electrode distance significantly influence this alignment by determining the electric field strength. During the alignment process, the applied electric field generates a torque needed to overcome the epoxy matrix's drag force, enabling CNT rotation and subsequent migration towards an electrode [12] Y. Minimizing the alignment time is an important factor to facilitate the large-scale fabrication of these aligned nanocomposites [14]. However, literature reports a wide disparity in these parameters—ranging from 10 V to 1000 V and distances of 1 mm to 50 mm—owing to variations in MWCNT type, epoxy viscosity, and system geometry [10], [11], [15]. While recent studies have leveraged RSM with ANOVA to optimize shear rate effects in MWCNT nanofluids along elongated surfaces [16] and employed Taguchi design for nitrogen-doped CNT synthesis [17], few have targeted the optimization of electric field parameters for minimizing CNT alignment time in epoxy matrix. This oversight limits the scalability and reproducibility of CNT/epoxy nanocomposite fabrication.

Rahman Julkarnyne M. Habibur · Gururaja Suhasini
Department of Aerospace Engineering, Auburn University, Auburn, AL 36849
e-mail: jzr0114@auburn.edu; suhasini.gururaja@auburn.edu

Emily Retzlaff et al. (eds.), *Mechanics of Additive & Advanced Manufacturing, Inverse Methods and Machine Learning, Vol. 5*, Conference Proceedings of the Society for Experimental Mechanics Series, https://doi.org/10.13052/9788743808312-2

In this work, a design of experiments approach integrating RSM and ANOVA has been adopted to optimize voltage and electrode distance for MWCNT alignment in the epoxy matrix. A CCD was utilized within the RSM framework to construct a systematic test matrix, incorporating critical process parameters: applied voltage, electrode distance, and MWCNT weight percentage. The response variable, alignment time, was experimentally determined for each condition outlined in the test matrix. Linear regression models were subsequently developed to map the relationship between input parameters and alignment time, enabling the identification of optimal process conditions. Additionally, ANOVA was performed to assess each parameter's statistical significance and interactions, elucidating their individual and combined effects on the alignment process.

Materials

Epon-862 (diglycidyl ether of bisphenol F) and EPIKURE curing agent W (bisphenol-F epoxy resin and an aromatic amine) purchased from Miller-Stephenson were used as the resin and hardener following manufacturers recommended ratio of 100:26.4. Amine-functionalized MWCNTs (length: 10∼30 μm, outside dia: 10∼20 nm) were sourced from MKnano. The MWCNT dimensions were confirmed via SEM. All the materials were used as received.

Nanocomposite Fabrication with Electric Field Alignment

The nanocomposite is fabricated following a systematic approach to ensure proper dispersion. Initially, CNTs were preheated at 105°C for 10 minutes to eliminate moisture. The required amount of preheated nanofillers was then added to the epoxy resin, and dispersion was performed using an overhead stirrer (ONiLAB Electric Overhead Stirrer) equipped with a propeller-shaped blade. The stirring process was conducted at approximately 1000 rpm for 4.5–5 hours at 80°C to achieve effective dispersion. Afterward, the curing agent (Epikure W) was introduced into the mixture, followed by additional stirring for 7 minutes. The mixture was then vacuum-degassed for 10 minutes to remove the entrapped air. Following the dispersion process, the nanocomposite mixture was maintained at 80°C in an oven before being transferred into a preheated silicone mold. The mold was rectangular, with dimensions of 180 mm × 40 mm (L × W), and was initially preheated in the oven to ensure uniform thermal conditions. Subsequently, the mold was placed on a hotplate set to 125°C, ensuring the mixture temperature remained around 80°C to maintain low viscosity during the alignment process. Two copper electrodes were positioned at a fixed distance and immersed in the nanocomposite mixture. An alternating current (AC) voltage was applied via a function generator coupled with a power amplifier to induce the alignment of carbon nanotubes (CNTs). The current was monitored with a digital multimeter throughout the alignment process to assess the progression of CNT movement. The voltage supply was discontinued after a predetermined duration, which depended on the applied voltage and electrode spacing. The mixture was then allowed to cool for 25 minutes before being transferred to an oven for curing. The curing process was conducted at 121°C for 2 hours, followed by post-curing at 177°C for 2 hours. Using this methodology, CNT/epoxy nanocomposites were fabricated with CNT weight fractions of 0.1, 0.2, and 0.3 wt.%. Figure 1 depicts the process flowchart.

Experimental Procedure

Three voltage levels of 500 V, 870 V, and 1000 V were used for these experiments. Distances of 50 mm, 75 mm, and 100 mm were used and combined with the mentioned voltage level to find the minimum alignment time. The frequency was fixed at 10 kHz. An RSM approach employing CCD was utilized to assess alignment time across various parameter combinations. Key process parameters—voltage, electrode distance, and CNT weight percentage (wt%)—served as experimental inputs (Table 1). The objective was to identify the optimal parameters yielding the minimum alignment time. The DOE approach reduced the experimental trials required while enabling analysis of voltage and distance effects on alignment time.

Table 1 Process parameters

Parameters	Code	Level of parameters		
Voltage (V)	A	500	870	1000
Distance (mm)	B	50	75	100
Weight percentage (wt%)	C	0.1	0.2	0.3

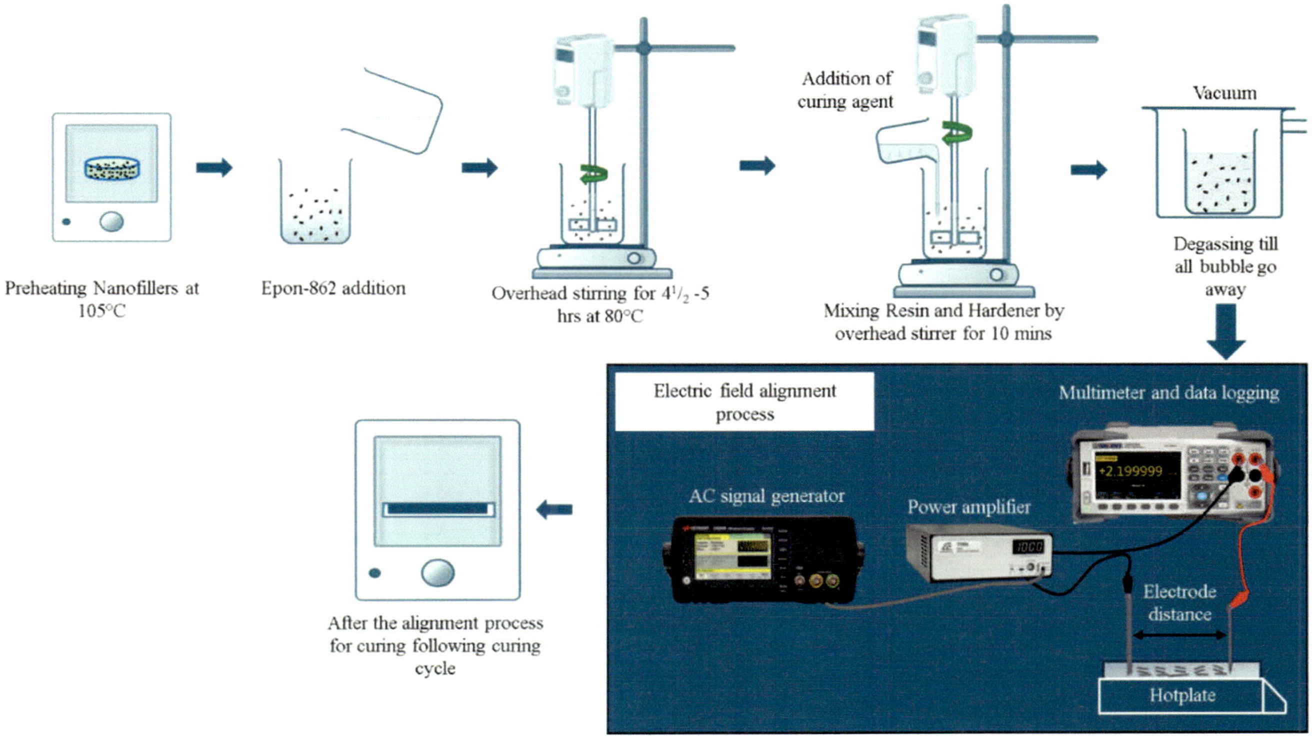

Fig. 1 Nanocomposite fabrication process with electric field alignment process

Results and Discussion

Using Stat-Ease 360 software, DOE tables were generated based on these inputs. Two experimental cases were considered for this approach. The first case involved only 0.1 wt.% CNT/epoxy, while the second case included 0.1, 0.2, and 0.3 wt.% CNT/epoxy. Table 2 presents the design matrix and corresponding output responses for 11 experimental runs in the first case, where voltage and distance were varied. Similarly, Table 3 details the design matrix and output responses for 15 experiments conducted under the second case based on the selected process parameters. In all these experiments, alignment time was monitored by measuring current (A) data from the multimeter. An empirical model was developed for both cases utilizing RSM. Following RSM implementation and identification of significant input parameters, ANOVA was performed to ensure the responses' statistical accuracy and validate the proposed model's suitability for predicting alignment time.

Table 2 Experiment matrix and obtained results for 0.1 CNT/Epoxy

	Factor 1	Factor 2	Response 1
Run	A: voltage (V)	B: Distance (mm)	Alignment time (min)
1	500	75	15
2	870	50	6
3	870	100	16
4	870	75	10
5	500	100	18
6	1000	50	3
7	1000	100	15
8	870	75	10
9	870	75	10
10	500	50	8
11	1000	75	12

Table 3 Experiment matrix and obtained results for different weight percentages (0.1, 0.2, 0.3 wt%)

	Factor 1	Factor 2	Factor 3	Response 1
Run	A: Voltage (V)	B: Distance (mm)	C: Weight percentage (wt%)	Alignment time(min)
1	870	100	0.1	16
2	870	50	0.1	6
3	500	75	0.1	15
4	870	75	0.1	10
5	1000	75	0.3	9
6	500	50	0.2	10
7	500	75	0.3	10
8	500	100	0.2	18
9	1000	100	0.2	10
10	500	50	0.1	8
11	870	50	0.3	10
12	1000	75	0.1	12
13	870	75	0.2	11
14	1000	50	0.1	3
15	870	100	0.3	14

Analysis for Alignment time

ANOVA for minimized alignment time has been represented in Tables 4 to 5, respectively. The F-value is a critical metric for identifying factors that significantly influence the physical quantity of interest. Specifically, a large F-value indicates that variations in a particular factor have a substantial impact on the observed output [17]. Table 4 shows that the model F-value of 54.93 indicates significant model performance, with only a 0.01% probability that such a high F-value is due to noise. P-values below 0.0500 denote significant model terms [18], specifically A and B, in this case.

Table 4 ANOVA for alignment time for 0.1 CNT/Epoxy

Source	Sum of Squares (SS)	df	Mean Square	F-value	p-value	Remarks & Percentage of Contribution (%)
Model	209.64	2	104.82	54.93	< 0.0001	
A-Voltage	28.14	1	28.14	14.75	0.0049	12.51 (significant)
B-Distance	181.50	1	181.50	95.12	< 0.0001	80.70
Residual	15.27	8	1.91			
Cor Total	224.91	10				
Std. Dev.	1.38			$\mathbf{R^2}$	0.9321	
Mean	11.09			Adjusted $\mathbf{R^2}$	0.9152	
Coefficient of variance (%)	12.45			Predicted $\mathbf{R^2}$	0.8652	
				Adequate precision	20.9609	

In Table 5, the Model F-value of 9.45 implies the model is significant, and there is only a 0.22% chance that an F-value this large could occur due to noise. Additionally, P-values less than 0.0500 indicate that model terms are significant. A (voltage) and B (distance) are significant model terms valid at 95% confidence in both cases. Additionally, the signal-to-noise ratio is evaluated using adequate precision measures, with a ratio exceeding four deemed desirable [16]. In Table 4, the adequate precision is 20.96, and in Table 5, it is 9.6, signifying both models are desirable and can be used to navigate the design space.

Figure 2 represents the normal plot of the residual for the alignment time. The residuals align closely along the normal line, indicating that the errors follow a normal distribution [18]. In both cases, the empirical model obtained for the output

Table 5 ANOVA for alignment time for different weight percentages of CNT/Epoxy

Source	Sum of Squares (SS)	df	Mean Square	F-value	p-value	Remarks& Percentage of Contribution (%)
Model	160.60	3	53.53	9.45	0.0022	
A-Voltage	40.65	1	40.65	7.17	0.0215	18.23
B-Distance	131.81	1	131.81	23.26	0.0005	59.13
C-Weight percentage	0.1124	1	0.1124	0.0198	0.8906	0.05
Residual	62.33	11	5.67			
Cor Total	222.93	14				
Std. Dev.	2.38			R^2	0.7204	
Mean	10.73			Adjusted R^2	0.6442	
Coefficient of variance (%)	22.18			Predicted R^2	0.4162	
				Adequate precision	9.6048	

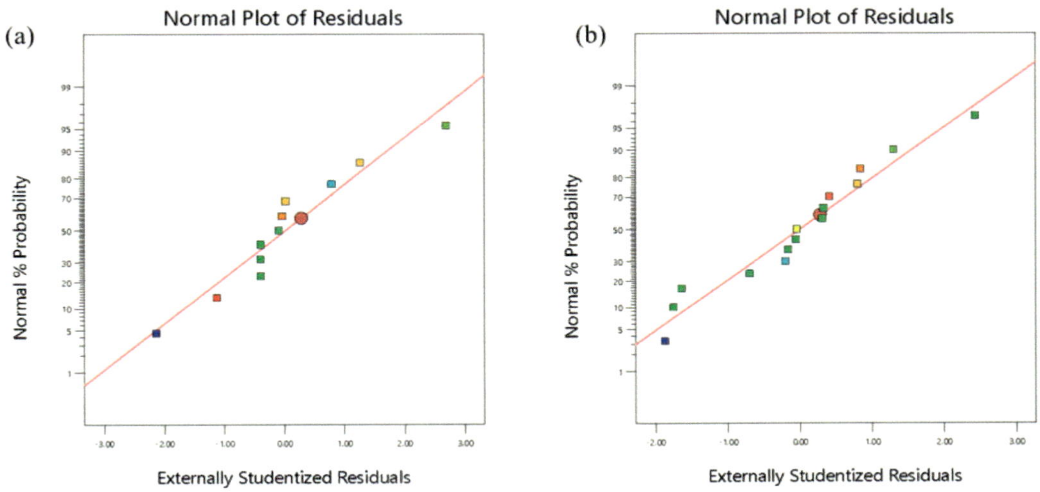

Fig. 2 Normal probabilities of residuals for (a) Alignment time using only 0.1 wt% CNT/Epoxy and (b) alignment time when different weight percentages of CNT used

was deemed effective at a 95% confidence level. The regression model for both cases factoring voltage and distance for the alignment time is presented in equations(1) and (2).

When the weight percentage is fixed at 0.1 wt% CNT, then the regression model of minimum alignment time is represented in equation (1)

$$\text{Alignment time} = 11.540 - 2.061^{*}A + 5.5^{*}B \quad \text{(Equation 1)}$$

When the weight percentage is varied between 0.1, 0.2, and 0.3 wt% CNT, then the regression model of minimum alignment time is represented in equation (2)

$$\text{Alignment time} = 11.22 - 2.017^{*}A + 3.939^{*}B - 0.106^{*}C \quad \text{(Equation 2)}$$

Where A represents the voltage, B represents the distance, and C represents the weight percentage of the CNT.

Multi-response optimization

The desirability function approach was employed for multi-response optimization to determine the optimal input process parameters. This method is widely utilized for optimizing both single- and multi-response problems. In this approach, each output response is converted into a dimensionless desirability index (D), ranging from 0 (least desirable) to 1 (most desirable). The optimal parameter set is identified when the corresponding solution achieves the highest overall desirability, ensuring the best possible outcome across multiple responses [18], [19]. In this study, the optimal values of voltage and distance are achieved after establishing the goal to minimize the alignment time. *Figure 3* represents the optimized bar histogram for desirability. Tables 6 and 7 present the constraints for the input parameters and the corresponding optimal solutions for minimizing alignment time. In both cases, the predicted optimal parameters were determined to be 1000 V and 50 mm, achieving the highest desirability score of 0.8. Furthermore, Table 8 compares the predicted and observed values of the process parameters to validate the model's accuracy. The average deviation between observed and predicted values is

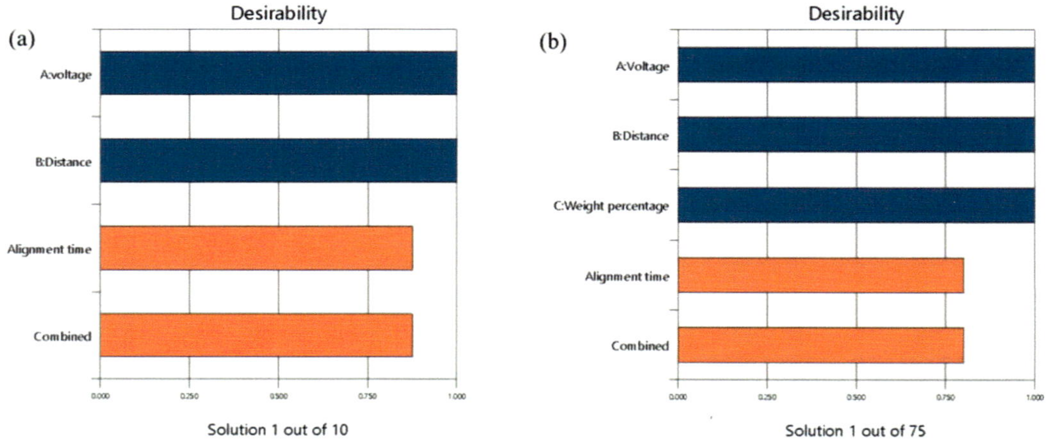

Fig. 3 Bar histogram demonstration for desirability (a) Alignment time using only 0.1 wt% CNT/Epoxy (b) alignment time when different weight percentages of CNT used

Table 6 Constraints and optimal solutions when weight percentage is fixed at 0.1 wt%

Name	Goal	Lower Limit	Upper Limit	Lower Weight	Upper Weight	Importance	Optimal solutions
A: Voltage	is in range	500.0	1000.0	1.0	1.0	3	1000
B: Distance	is in range	50.0	100.0	1.0	1.0	3	50
Alignment time	minimize	2.0	18.0	1.0	1.0	3	3.980

Table 7 Constraints and optimal solutions when weight percentage is varied

Name	Goal	Lower Limit	Upper Limit	Lower Weight	Upper Weight	Importance	Optimal solutions
A: Voltage	is in range	500.0	1000.0	1.0	1.0	3	1000
B: Distance	is in range	50.0	100.0	1.0	1.0	3	50
C: Weight percentage	is in range	0.1	0.3	1.0	1.0	3	0.3
Alignment time	minimize	2.0	18.0	1.0	1.0	3	5.165

Table 8 Observed and predicted results at optimum values of process parameters

Voltage (V)	Distance (mm)	Weight percentage (wt%)	Alignment time (Predicted by model)	Alignment time (Experimental value)
870	75	0.1	10.35	10
500	50	0.1	9	8
1000	75	0.3	9.15	9
1000	100	0.2	13.15	15
500	100	0.2	17.18	18

approximately 0.83, demonstrating the model's reliability in predicting alignment time for different voltage and distance combinations.

Effect of Process Parameters on Alignment Time

From the ANOVA results (Table 4, Table 5), it can be observed that both voltage and distance play a significant role in minimizing alignment time. The percentage of contribution ratio (PCR) of each input parameter can quantify the effect and the interaction of those parameters. The PCR in both tables is calculated by dividing the sum of squares (SS) for each factor by the total SS [17]. As shown in Table 4, the electrode distance contributes 80.70% to minimizing the alignment time for 0.1 wt.% CNT/Epoxy, whereas the applied voltage accounts for only 12.51%. Similarly, Table 5 presents the percentage contribution ratios (PCRs) for varying CNT weight fractions, indicating that distance and voltage contribute 59.13% and 18.23%, respectively, to reduce alignment time. These findings highlight the dominant influence of electrode distance over voltage in optimizing the alignment process. The ANOVA results indicate that electrode distance is the primary factor influencing alignment time. This is attributed to its significant impact on the electric field strength, which plays a crucial role in facilitating the formation of an aligned conductive network under the applied AC electric field [9], [10]. With the decrease in distance and the increase in voltage, the electric field strength increased which eventually increased the torque that facilitates the alignment of the CNT in the electric field direction[20]. In addition to the ANOVA results, the initial test matrix (Tables 1 and 2) highlights that a lower electrode distance and higher applied voltage enhance the electric field strength, thereby influencing alignment time. However, excessively high voltages can induce CNT aggregation, leading to the formation of rope-like structures, which may adversely impact the nanocomposite's properties [13].

As shown in Table 5, the weight percentage of CNTs has a minimal effect on reducing alignment time, with a PCR of only 0.05%. However, in practice, CNT weight percentage does influence alignment time. A higher CNT concentration provides more conductive pathways, facilitating alignment under the applied voltage compared to lower concentrations [10].

Conclusions

This study demonstrates the efficacy of integrating RSM and ANOVA to optimize voltage and electrode distance for minimizing the MWCNT alignment time in the epoxy matrix.

- Higher voltage and shorter distance significantly enhance alignment efficiency.
- Future work will involve COMSOL simulations to further investigate the effects of viscosity and epoxy curing dynamics, refining alignment kinetics, and paving the way for industrial scalability.
- The study will be extended to optimize the voltage and distance for the GNP/Epoxy sample in the future.

References

1. Kota, AK, "Commentary: Polymer/carbon-nanotube nanocomposites: from innovation to commercialization," JNP, vol. 3, no. 1, p. 030307, Sep. 2009,
2. Zhang, D, Huang, Y, and Chia, L, "Effects of carbon nanotube (CNT) geometries on the dispersion characterizations and adhesion properties of CNT reinforced epoxy composites," Composite Structures, vol. 296, p. 115942, Sep. 2022,
3. Shen, M-Y, Liao, W-Y, Wang, T-Q, and Lai, W-M, "Characteristics and Mechanical Properties of Graphene Nanoplatelets-Reinforced Epoxy Nanocomposites: Comparison of Different Dispersal Mechanisms," Sustainability, vol. 13, no. 4, Art. no. 4, Jan. 2021,
4. Pothnis, JR, Kalyanasundaram, D, and Gururaja, S, "Mitigation of notch sensitivity by controlled alignment of carbon nanotubes in epoxy using electric field application," Composites Part A: Applied Science and Manufacturing, vol. 149, no. 2021, p. 106544, Oct. 2021,
5. Moaseri, E, Fotouhi, M, Bazubandi, B, Karimi, M, Baniadam, M, and Maghrebi, M, "Two-dimensional reinforcement of epoxy composites: alignment of multi-walled carbon nanotubes in two directions," Advanced Composite Materials, vol. 29, no. 6, pp. 547–557, Nov. 2020,
6. Moaseri, E, Karimi, M, Bazubandi, B, Baniadam, M, and Maghrebi, M, "Alignment of Carbon Nanotubes in Bulk Epoxy Matrix using a Magnetic-Assisted Method: Solenoid Magnetic Field 1," Polymer Science, Series A, vol. 59, no. 5, pp. 726–733, 2017,
7. Wu, S, Ladani, RB, Zhang, J, Bafekrpour, E, Ghorbani, K, Mouritz, AP, Kinloch, AJ, and Wang, CH, "Aligning multilayer graphene flakes with an external electric field to improve multifunctional properties of epoxy nanocomposites," Carbon, vol. 94, pp. 607–618, Nov. 2015,
8. Felisberto, M, Arias-Durán, A, Ramos, JA, Mondragon, I, Candal, R, Goyanes, S, and Rubiolo, GH, "Influence of filler alignment in the mechanical and electrical properties of carbon nanotubes/epoxy nanocomposites," Physica B: Condensed Matter, vol. 407, no. 16, pp. 3181–3183, Aug. 2012,

9. Pothnis, JR, Kalyanasundaram, D, and Gururaja, S, "Controlled manipulation of CNTs in glass/epoxy composites with cut-outs using non-uniform electric field," Advanced Composite Materials, vol. 30, no. 2021, pp. 205–221, 2020,
10. Khan, SU, Pothnis, JR, and Kim, JK, "Effects of carbon nanotube alignment on electrical and mechanical properties of epoxy nanocomposites," Composites Part A: Applied Science and Manufacturing, vol. 49, pp. 26–34, Jun. 2013,
11. Oliva-Avilés, AI, Avilés, F, Sosa, V, Oliva, AI, and Gamboa, F, "Dynamics of carbon nanotube alignment by electric fields," Nanotechnology, vol. 23, no. 46, p. 465710, Nov. 2012,
12. Monti, M, Natali, M, Torre, L, and Kenny, JM, "The alignment of single walled carbon nanotubes in an epoxy resin by applying a DC electric field," Carbon, vol. 50, no. 7, pp. 2453–2464, Jun. 2012,
13. Amani, AM, Hashemi, SA, Mousavi, SM, Abrishamifar, SM, Vojood, A, Amani, AM, Hashemi, SA, Mousavi, SM, Abrishamifar, SM, and Vojood, A, "Electric Field Induced Alignment of Carbon Nanotubes: Methodology and Outcomes," in Carbon Nanotubes - Recent Progress, IntechOpen, 2017.
14. Zhu, Y-F, Ma, C, and Zhang, W, "Alignment of multiwalled carbon nanotubes in bulk epoxy composites via electric field," J. Appl. Phys, vol. 105, p. 54319, 2009,
15. Pothnis, JR, Gururaja, S, and Kalyanasundaram, D, "Mechanics of Advanced Materials and Structures Development and characterization of electric field directed preferentially aligned CNT nanocomposites," 2019,
16. Baithalu, R and Mishra, SR, "On optimizing shear rate analysis for the water-based CNT micropolar nanofluids via an elongating surface: response surface methodology combined with ANOVA test," J Therm Anal Calorim, vol. 148, no. 24, pp. 14275–14294, Dec. 2023,
17. Silva, RM, Fernandes, AJS, Ferro, MC, Pinna, N, and Silva, RF, "Vertically aligned N-doped CNTs growth using Taguchi experimental design," Applied Surface Science, vol. 344, pp. 57–64, Jul. 2015,
18. Kumar, D and Gururaja, S, "Abrasive waterjet machining of Ti/CFRP/Ti laminate and multi-objective optimization of the process parameters using response surface methodology," Journal of Composite Materials, vol. 54, no. 13, pp. 1741–1759, Jun. 2020,
19. Dhanawade, A and Kumar, S, "Experimental study of delamination and kerf geometry of carbon epoxy composite machined by abrasive water jet," Journal of Composite Materials, vol. 51, no. 24, pp. 3373–3390, Oct. 2017,
20. Du, JR, Zheng, J, Ma, K, Du, C, and Zhou, D, "Electric Field-induced Orientation of Carbon Nanomaterials in Dispersions," ChemistrySelect, vol. 9, no. 6, p. e202303547, 2024,

Chapter 3
Interfacial Characterization of Metal Wire Inlays for 3D Printed FDM Parts

Vereesh Ayyagari, Hugh A. Bruck, Amir H. Ohadi, and Michael M. Ohadi

Abstract A novel process for creating 3D printed parts with metal wire inlay has been developed at the University of Maryland. By using metal wire inlay, parts can retain the properties of drawn metal wires that can be either embedded in polymer or fully exposed. As a result, the mechanical integrity of the metal wire interface with the FDM polymer can be controlled through the printing conditions and preparation of the wire surface. In this investigation, we develop a novel test specimen for characterizing the mechanical integrity of the metal wire/polymer interface. In particular, the test specimen is designed to quantify the ability of the interface to provide hermetic sealing when loaded by pressurized fluids. The effects of the processing and preparation conditions on the interfacial strength are also investigated via single fiber pullout tests. As a result, it is possible to design new 3D-printed metal-polymer composite structures with free standing metal wires that can be utilized in a a variety of different applications ranging from integrated flow sensing to enhanced thermal control.

Keywords Metal-polymer composites · Polymer-metal interface · Failure characterization · Adhesion · Interfacial strength

Introduction

Polymer matrix-metal wire composite structures are increasingly being developed for strengthening polymer structures [1], heat exchangers [2], and conductive path tracing for electronic components [3]. For a mechanistic point of view, there could be two variants of the composites. In the first, the metal wire is wholly embedded in the polymer. In the second composite, the metal wires are partially exposed, resulting in a partially free-standing metal wire. The two variants of the composites are shown in **Figure 1,** where Figure 1a shows the polymer-metal composites where the metal wires are completely embedded into the polymer, and 1b shows the composites where metal wires are partially free-standing.

While the fabrication of the composite can be achieved through conventional manufacturing techniques, additive manufacturing, commonly referred to as 3D Printing, has become popular choice of fabrication, primarily due to the complex nature of the composite. For 3D printing of the composites, Fused Filament Fabrication (FFF) has been widely used for depositing the polymer, and metal wires are thermally embedded. In FFF, thermoplastic materials, such as polycarbonates, acrylonitrile butadiene styrene (ABS), Polylactic Acid (PLA), and Poly Amides (PA), are used as feedstocks due to their favorable properties such as low melting temperature and appropriate melt viscosities [4]. Recently, we have developed a 3D printing process for metal wire-inlay to create cross-media heat exchangers [5–8] which contains an array of free-standing metal wires embedded into the polymer structure.

The failure mechanisms of the polymer-metal composites are critical to understanding their limitations in the applications. In particular, to estimate how much pressure can be applied to the structure before the wires start pulling out i.e. interfacial strength between metal and polymer, wire push out tests are applied [1, 9–11]. While a few studies exist on the characterization of composites where metal fibers that are embedded continuously in a polymer matrix, very few have studied 3D-printed polymer-metal composites fundamentally, where the metal wires are partially exposed. The current study focuses on the failure characterization of the partially free-standing metal fibers in polymer-metal composites.

Vereesh Ayyagari · Hugh A. Bruck · Amir H. Ohadi · Michael M. Ohadi
Department of Mechanical Engineering, A. James Clark School of Engineering, University of Maryland, College Park, MD 20742
e-mail: veeresha@umd.edu; bruck@umd.edu; amir@umd.edu; ohadi@umd.edu

Emily Retzlaff et al. (eds.), *Mechanics of Additive & Advanced Manufacturing, Inverse Methods and Machine Learning, Vol. 5*,
Conference Proceedings of the Society for Experimental Mechanics Series, https://doi.org/10.13052/9788743808312-3

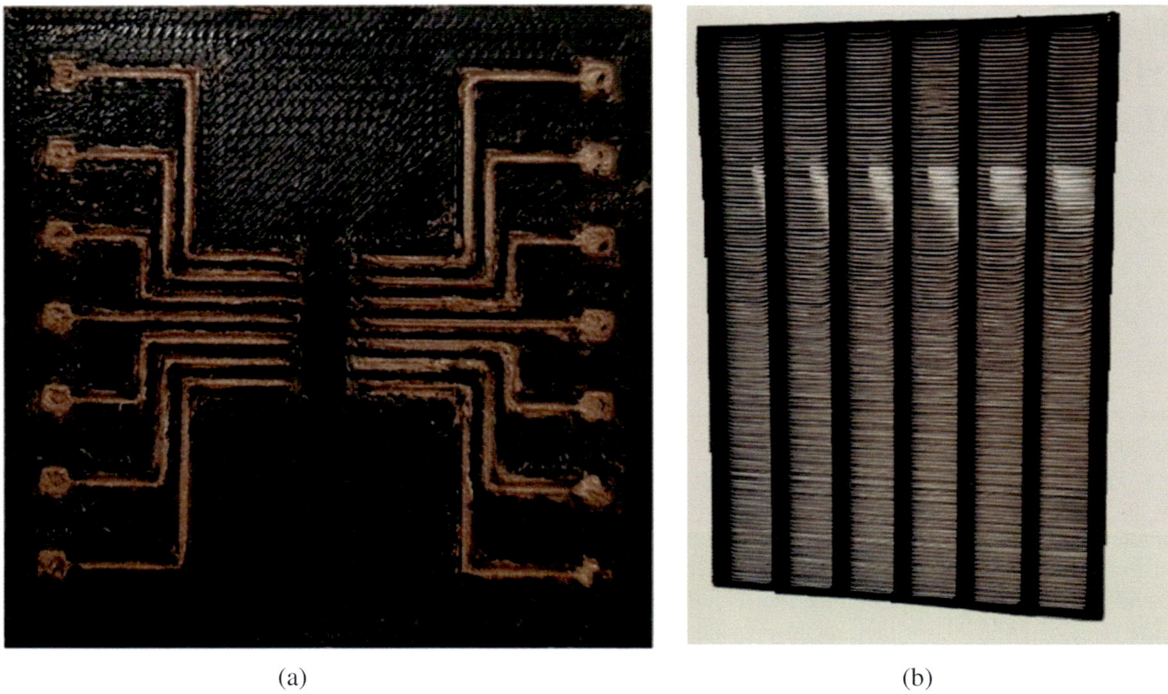

Fig. 1 The variants of polymer-metal composites: (a) continuously embedded metal fiber in the polymer [6], and (b) Partially embedded metal fibers in the polymer [2]

Specimen Fabrication and Testing

Polymer matrix-metal wire composites can be used as functional structures in a variety of applications requiring the conductivity of metal and the lightweight provided by polymer supports (e.g., lightweight heat exchangers). In many applications, the polymer structure may be pressurized, such as by a working fluid in a heat exchanger and may be subject to a differential pressure that may cause a partially free-standing metal wire to pull out of the polymer support structure. For this investigation, a specimen was designed and fabricated that allowed for testing of multiple partially free-standing wires embedded in a polymer structure that is subjected to a differential pressure (i.e., a polymer pressure vessel with metal stringers). The cross-section of the composite specimen that was fabricated and tested in this investigation can be seen in Figure 2.

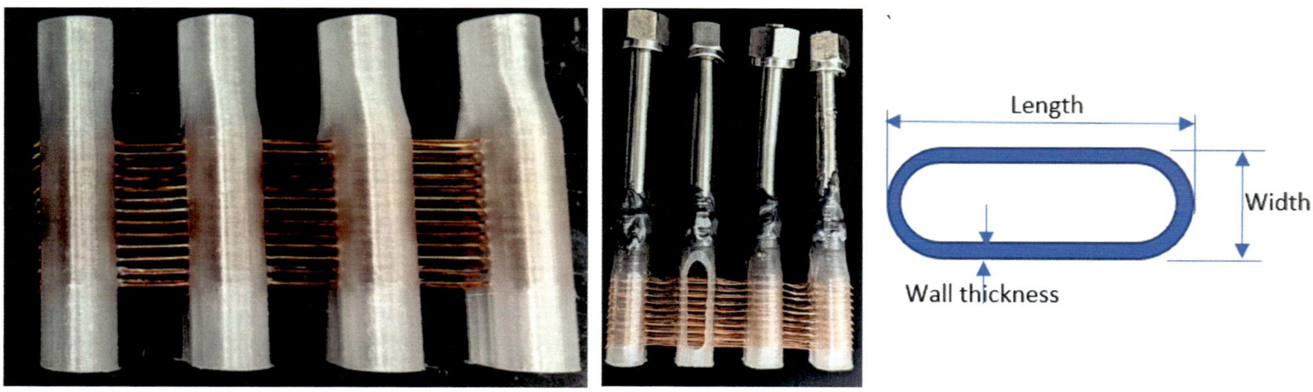

Fig. 2 (left) Cross-media coupons (middle) Cross-sectioned coupon exposing free-standing wires inside (right) The geometrical parameters of the cross-media coupons as seen from top cross-section view

To maintain its integrity in applications where the polymer structure is pressurized, the composite structure should not leak at the metal wire/polymer interface during operation, i.e. maintain the sealing in pressurized condition. Currently, there is no standard available for determining the maximum pressure limit for this type of specimen. Therefore, to obtain the pressure at which the leakage happens for different geometries, specimens were fabricated and tested using polycarbonate as the polymer, and copper wires as the metal fibers.

Specimen Fabrication: To fabricate specimens, an off-the-shelf polymer 3D printer was customized to embed metal fibers over the polymer layers with a proprietary metal fiber print head, shown in **Figure 3**. To facilitate the visualization of the metal wire/polymer matrix failure (i.e. leakage), clear polycarbonate was chosen as the polymer and copper as the metal. The coupons as printer were found to be leaking near the metal-polymer interface. To avoid this leakage, the composite was dip-coated in a commercially procured 3d print sealer, an epoxy-hardener mixture, and cured in an oven at 50 °C for 24 hours. A post-curing regimen was followed where the cured coupons were kept in an oven at 90 °C for 2 hours and allowed to cool in the oven slowly to minimize residual stresses.

UMD TAZ Printer

Proprietary Metal Fiber Print Head

Fig. 3 (left) A 3D FDM printer customized at UMD for metal wire inlay using (right) a proprietary metal fiber print head.

Two different types of cross-media coupons were tested for failure. All coupons had the same geometrical parameters except for wall thickness. The vertical and horizontal pitches were maintained the same in all coupons. The geometrical parameters of the cross-media coupons are mentioned in Table 1.

Table 1 Geometrical parameters of the cross-media coupons

Parameter	Value	
	Coupon-1	Coupon-2
Wall thickness (mm)	1.8	3
Length (mm)	20	
Width (mm)	11.5	
Wire diameter (mm)	0.5	
Vertical wire pitch (mm)	3	
Horizontal wire pitch (mm)	2.6	

All coupons after the post-curing were tested for leakage at 50 PSI using a bubble test. Only the coupons that passed the bubble test were used for failure characterization. For failure characterization, a pressure decay method was used. The schematic of the experimental setup is shown in **Figure 4**. To pressurize the coupon, an Additel 925 hydraulic pressure test pump was used. Once the unit under test (UUT) reaches the required pressure, the needle valve is closed to shutoff the UUT from the pump and allow for pressure decay. To record the pressure in the coupon a pressure gauge is connected between the valve and the UUT. A DAQ was connected to the pressure gauge to collect the pressure data every second to monitor the pressure decay.

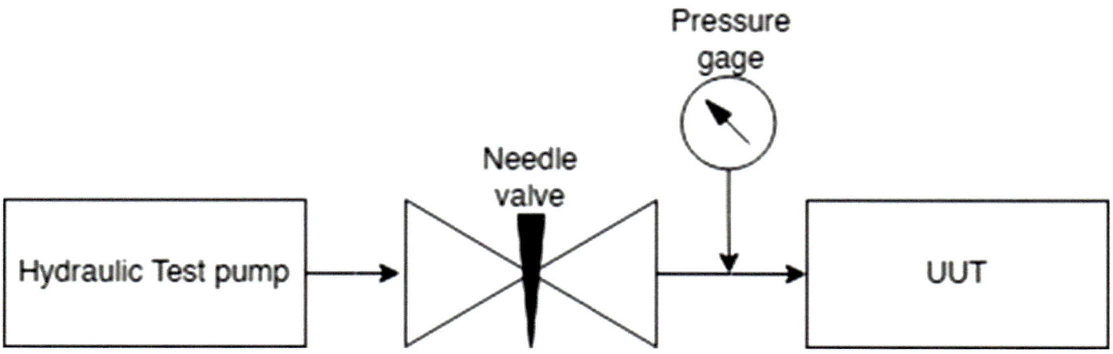

Fig. 4 Pressure decay test schematic

Experimental Results

Three specimens with the desired test geometry were fabricated and tested, as well as another two specimens that had slightly thicker polymer support, The resulting variation of pressure with time for one of the specimens with the thinner polymer supports is shown in **Figure 5**. The pressure decay test started at 50 PSI and was held for 10 minutes before being increased in 25 psi steps holding 10 minutes between steps, and was carried out at 25 PSI increments. At each pressure level, the UUT was shut off from the pump to obtain the pressure decay rate. At 275 psi, a water droplet was observed on the outer surface of the specimen at the metal wire/polymer matrix interface, indicating leakage, which was considered a catastrophic failure and ended the test. A similar testing protocol was carried out on two other specimens and three samples of coupon2 and the pressure decay rate at each pressure level is reported in **Figure 6**. As seen from the figure, until 150 PSI, the pressure decay rate stays relatively constant. However, the decay rate increases significantly with further increases in pressure above 150 PSI. This transition point at 150 PSI indicates that it should be considered the pressure limit. Additionally, the decay rates are different for each step above 150 PSI, which could potentially be attributed to the number of failure locations, since there are multiple metal wire/polymer support interfaces. For the second specimen geometry, the pressure decay rate transition

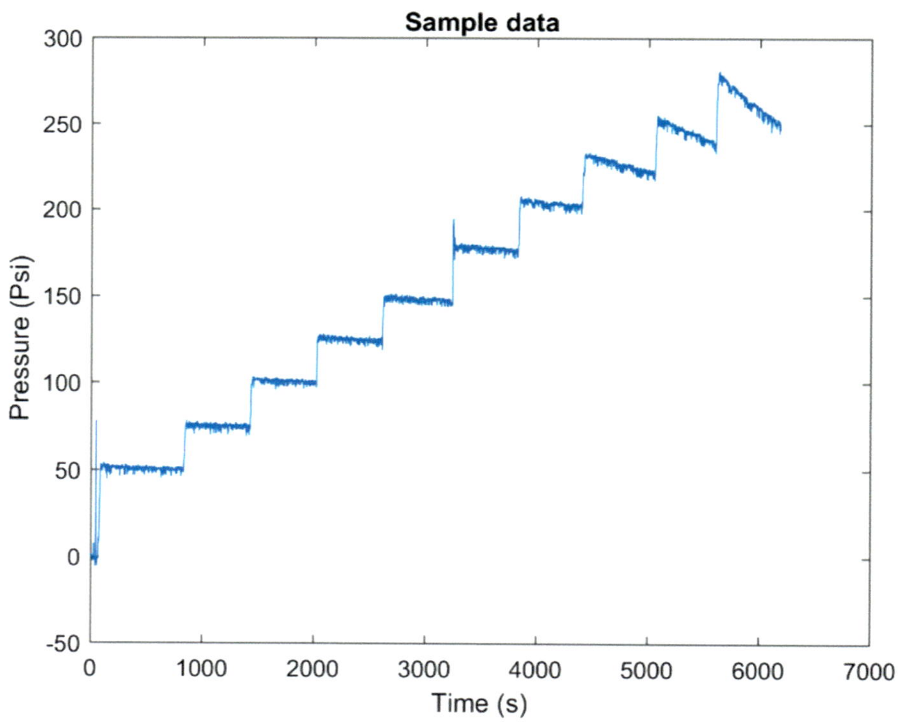

Fig. 5 Pressure decay test on the first sample from coupon 1, coupon-1-1

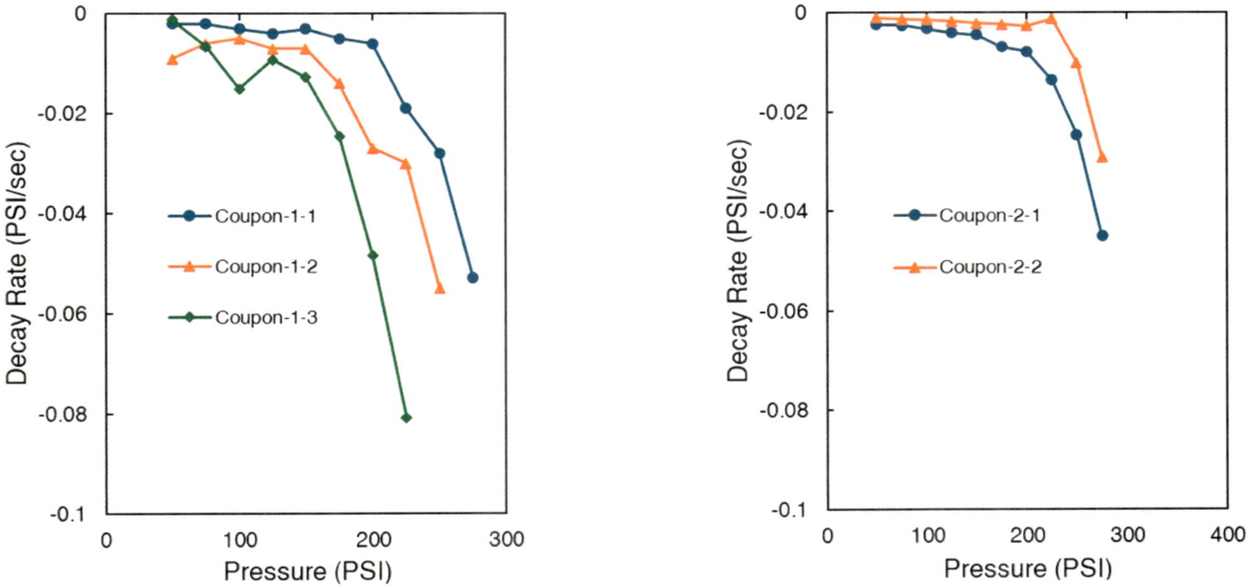

Fig. 6 Pressure decay rate vs. pressure for coupon-1 and coupon-2

point occurs at or above 200 PSI. This increase in the pressure limit could be attributed to increased wall thickness in the second specimen geometry.

Adhesion Characterization of Polymer-metal Interface

Single fiber pullout experiments

In order to characterize the adhesion of the polymer-metal interface, standard single fiber pullout experiments were performed. To better duplicate the actual embed conditions for the fibers, single wire specimens were prepared with wall geometries that were similar to those that were going to be used in real structures, such as polymer heat exchangers (PHXs). Therefore, a single metal fiber was embedded into printed polymer ends that had 1mm thick walls in various polymers, such as PETG, Tritan, and glass fiber infused PETG (**Figure 7**). One end of the specimen was printed as a 25 mm × 20 mm × 5

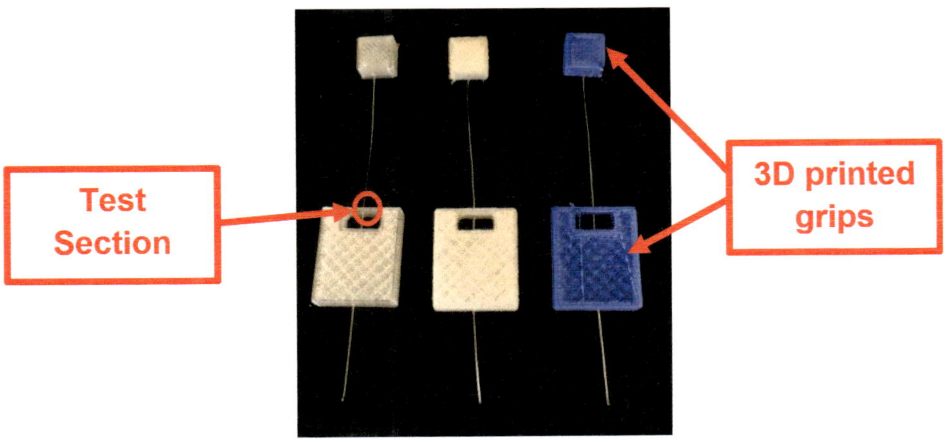

Fig. 7 Single Fiber Pull Out Test specimens with test section consisting of 1 mm thick polymer wall and a gap to cut and release the wire for pullout testing. From left to right are the various polymers we have successfully used to print test specimens: (a) PETG, (b) ABS, and (c) glass fiber infused PETG.

mm grip with a 5 mm gap and a 1 mm wall thickness on one side of the gap, which was chosen so that it mirrors a typical wall thickness used for an end application, such as a heat exchanger. The free-standing wire across the gap is cut to release the resistance from the length embedded into the grip, resulting in a gage length of 25 mm for the remaining free-standing portion of the wire, which has a diameter of 0.4 mm. A 4043 aluminum wire in the annealed condition was used.

The single fiber pullout tests can be performed for a variety of materials using a number of manufacturing techniques. These tests supported the development of a print head that uses both heat and mechanical force to embed the metal fibers and optimize adhesion. Preliminary investigations found very low bond strengths found when the fibers were placed into the print at room temperature, which necessitated improving the processing conditions for embedding the wire. These tests also focused more on PETG as a polymer of interest because of its ease of use and extremely high bond strengths are attractive for many potential applications, such as heat exchangers. The load-displacement results can be seen in **Figure 8** for a specimen that was printed with the wire heated to 175 °C and a nozzle temperature of 238 °C fot the glass fiber filled PETG. Note, the maximum load would produce a stress of 135 MPa in the metal wire, which exceeds the strength of the metal wire. Thus, the metal wire begins to draw out plastically before localized tensile failure occurs. Therefore, the performance is not limited by the interfacial strength, but rather the tensile strength of the metal wire.

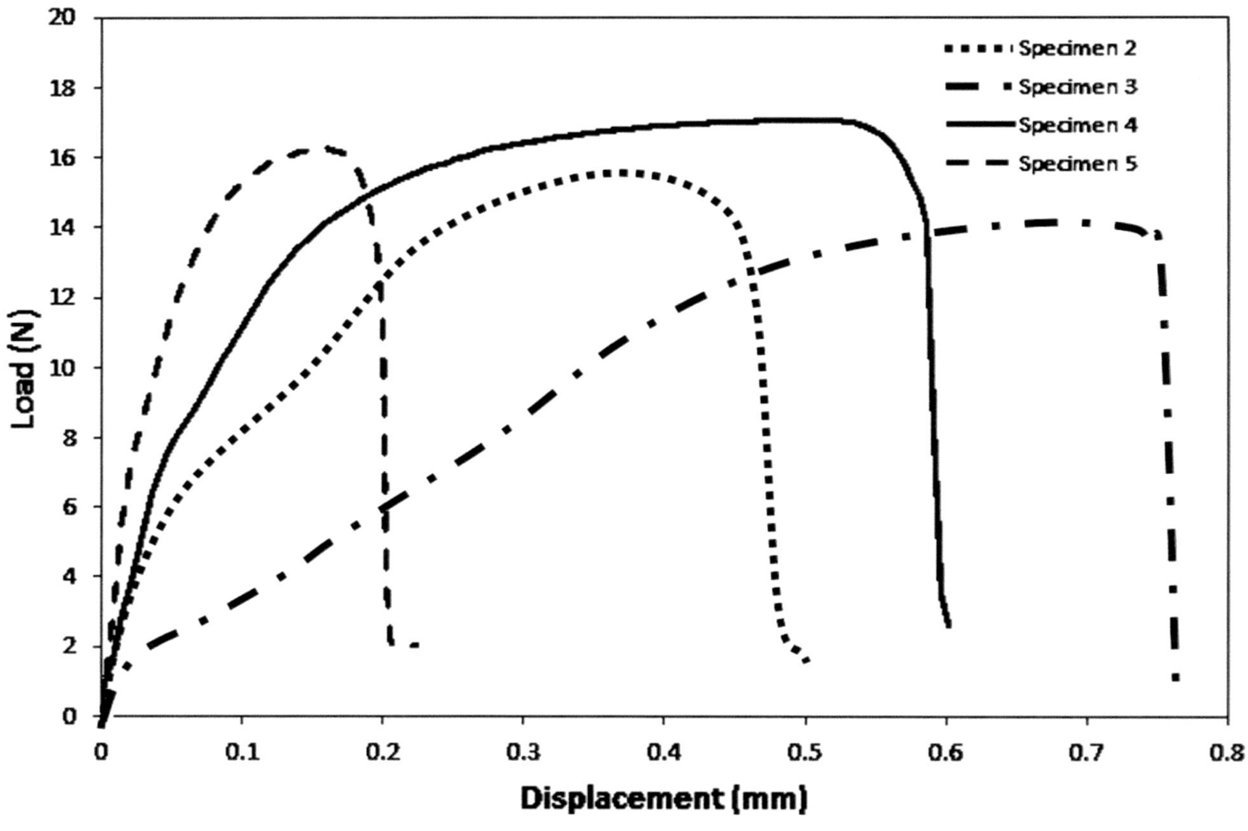

Fig. 8 (left) Load-displacement results for single fiber pullout specimens using metal wires embedded under optimal processing conditions that produced a shear strength that exceeded that need to initiate tensile failure of the metal wire (right).

Thermal characterization of FDM material during processing

A critical aspect of the wire inlay process is the effects of changing over from the FDM print head to the wire inlay head. During that time, the cooling of the FDM material changes the wetting and adhesion of the interface as the material undergoes transition from the melt to the solid phase. To better understand the effects of the state of the FDM material on the strength of the polymer-metal interface, it was necessary to characterize the thermal evolution of the FDM material during processing.

To characterize the thermal evolution of the material, thermocouple measurements were obtained in situ. Results can be seen in **Figure 9** for ABS. The thermal inertia of the thermocouple resulted in a peak temperature 8 seconds after deposition. However, the temperature did plateau at 100 °C, which is near the glass transition temperature of ABS, for another 12 seconds, before undergoing convective cooling. The temperature rapidly decays for another 60 seconds to approximately 40 °C, before reaching nearly steady state conditions associated with the bed temperature of the printer. It is during this 60 second period that the material undergoes phase transformations controlled by the convective cooling rate, which impacts the flow of the polymer at the wire surface, and the subsequent adhesion that develops as the polymer hardens. Therefore, mechanical characterization was conducted, to determine the sensitivity of inlaying the wire at different times on the level of adhesion.

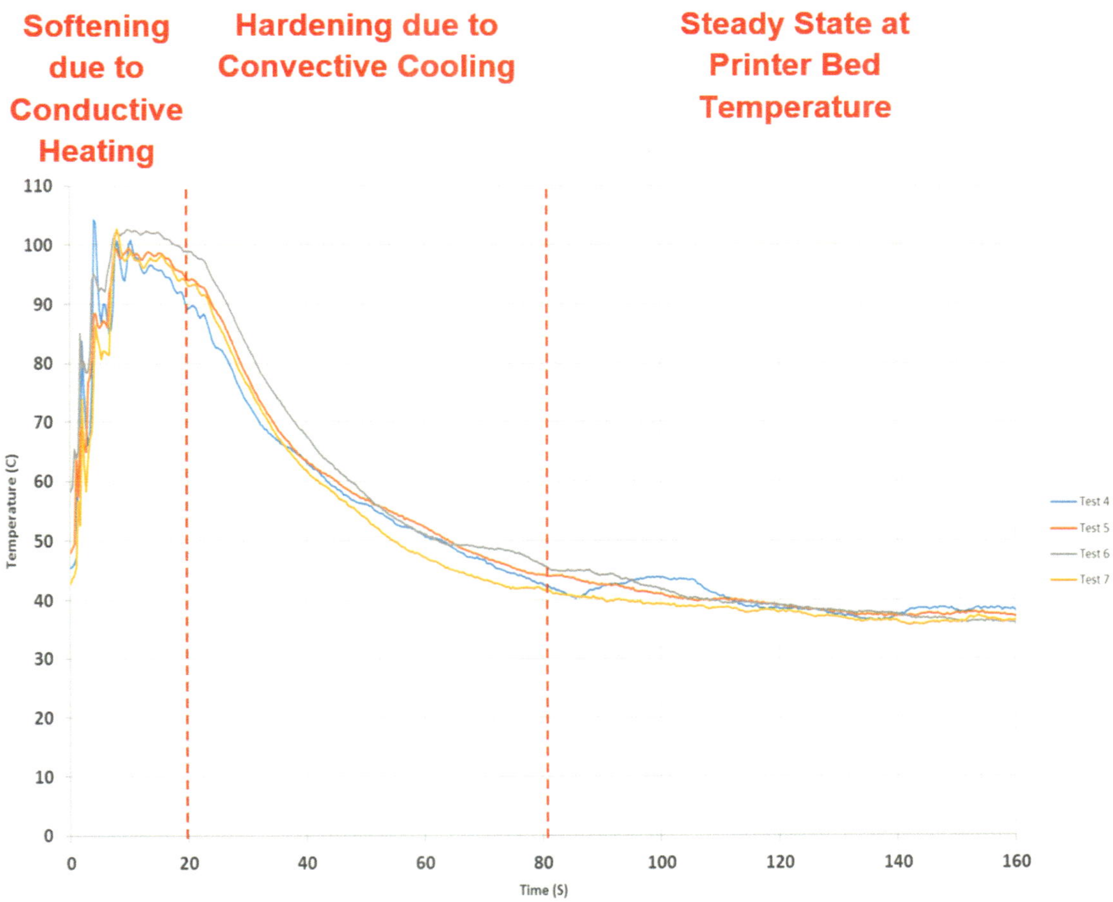

Fig. 9 Thermal evolution of FDM material during the printing process used to determine the time range in which to investigate the effect of inlaying the metal wire on adhesion, where the polymer cools to a steady state temperature of 40 °C with 60 seconds after deposition.

Mechanical characterization of metal wire/polymer support matrix interface for different processing conditions

Representative load-displacement results for the single fiber pullout specimens consisting of the aluminum wire inlayed onto ABS can be seen up until the ultimate load in **Figure 10**. Wire inlay times of 25 sec and 60 sec after the time for the control specimen were also investigated, as well as the use of abrasively polishing the metal wire to remove contaminants and promote adhesion. From these results, it can be seen that the interfacial strength is sufficient to permit the wire to begin to deform plastically, as with the glass fiber-filled PETG. A statistical comparison of the yield and ultimate loads obtained from these curves can be seen **Figure 11.**. It can be seen that the polished surface had a slightly higher ultimate loads than the unpolished for all inlay times, with the ultimate load being nearly twice the yield for the polished control specimens. However, the load for 25 s inlay times were 50% lower than the control with no signs of yielding, and the inlay at 50s resulted in a similar reduction relative to 25 s. This is not unexpected, since as the polymer is in a less viscous phase for adhesion, with the reduction being approximately proportional to the temperature at the inlay time relative to the difference between the initial melt temperature and the final bed temperature of the printer.

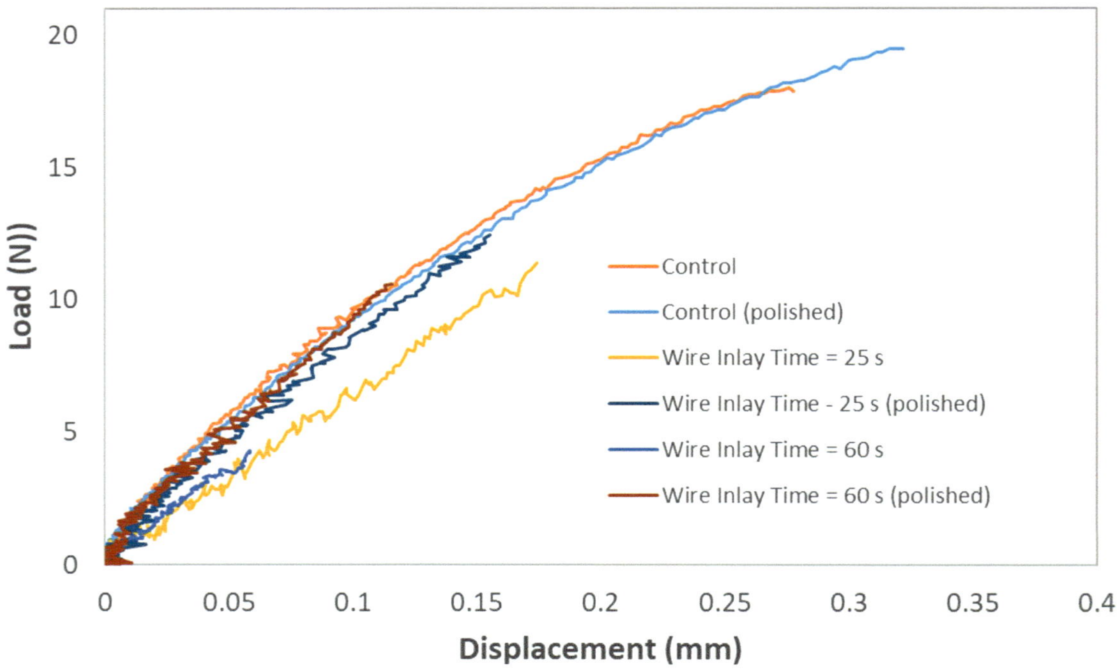

Fig. 10 Representative load-displacement curves for single fiber pullout specimens with polished and unpolished metal wires inlaid at different times relative to the control specimens.

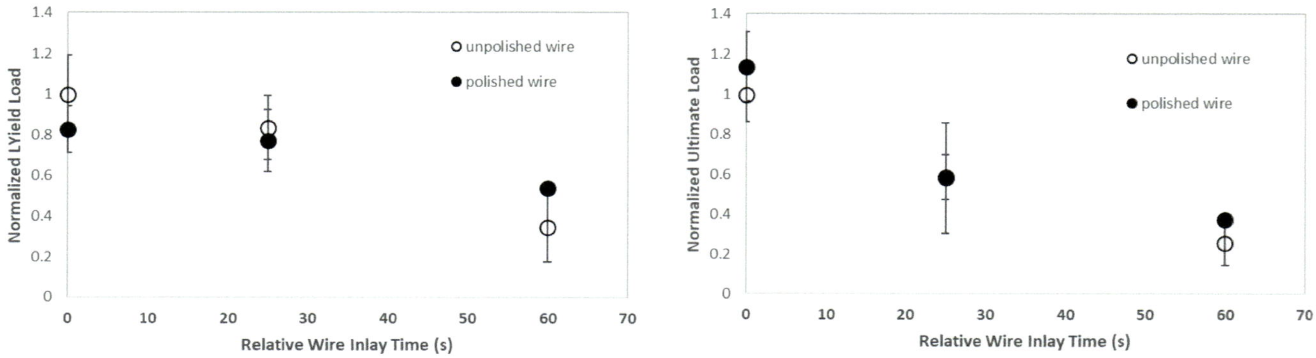

Fig. 11 Statistical comparison of average (left) yield fand (right) ultimate loads normalized by the average values of the control specimens, as well as their corresponding standard deviations for single fiber pullout specimens with polished and unpolished wires inlaid at different times relative to control specimens.

Conclusions

The development of 3D printed polymer composite structures with partially free-standing wires embedded in them is affording new opportunities to develop conductive structures that are optimized for lighter weight in a variety of applications, such as heat exchangers. However, there are new challenges in fabricating them to be with enough integrity at the metal wire/polymer matrix interface that they can withstand operating conditions involving pressure differentials that can cause the wires to pullout out and leakage to occur. In this investigation, we have developed a test specimen for characterizing the integrity of the metal wire/polymer matrix interface. The specimen was a small polymer pressure vessel that had multiple partially free-standing metal wires embedded in the walls. These specimens could then be pressurized to determine the loading which the metal wire/polymer matrix interface would fail. Pressures up to 150 psi could be sustained without failure, and up to 200 psi if the wall thickness is increased. Fiber pullout test specimens were also fabricated to determine the interfacial strength. It was determined that optimal conditions could be obtained using heated wires, although the adhesion was determined to reduce relative to the inlay time for the metal wire, up until the bed temperature of the printer is reached 60 seconds after deposition of the polymer melt. This was attributed to the polymer hardening and not being able to flow sufficiently at the wire surface in order to form good adhesive contact with the wire.

Acknowledgments Financial support of this work by the U.S. Department of Energy, ARPA-E division, under award number DE- AR0000584 is gratefully acknowledged. The views and opinions of authors expressed herein do not state or reflect those of the United States Government or any agency thereof.

References

1. C. Thompson, C. González, J. LLorca, Material extrusion fabrication of continuous metal wire-reinforced polymer–matrix composites, Composites Communications 50 (2024) 102024. bibhttps://doi.org/10.1016/j.coco.2024.102024.
2. M. Arie, D. Hymas, F. Singer, A. Shooshtari, M. Ohadi, Performance Characterization of a Novel Cross-Media Composite Heat Exchanger for Air-to-Liquid Applications, in: 2019 18th IEEE Intersociety Conference on Thermal and Thermomechanical Phenomena in Electronic Systems (ITherm), IEEE, 2019: pp. 933–940. bibhttps://doi.org/10.1109/ITHERM.2019.8757258.
3. H. Nassar, R. Dahiya, Fused Deposition Modeling-Based 3D-Printed Electrical Interconnects and Circuits, Advanced Intelligent Systems 3 (2021). bibhttps://doi.org/10.1002/aisy.202100102.
4. S. Park, W. Shou, L. Makatura, W. Matusik, K. (Kelvin) Fu, 3D printing of polymer composites: Materials, processes, and applications, Matter 5 (2022) 43–76. bibhttps://doi.org/10.1016/j.matt.2021.10.018.
5. M.A. Arie, D.M. Hymas, F. Singer, A.H. Shooshtari, M. Ohadi, An additively manufactured novel polymer composite heat exchanger for dry cooling applications, Int J Heat Mass Transf 147 (2020). bibhttps://doi.org/10.1016/j.ijheatmasstransfer.2019.118889.
6. M.A. Arie, D.M. Hymas, F. Singer, A.H. Shooshtari, M. Ohadi, An additively manufactured novel polymer composite heat exchanger for dry cooling applications, Int J Heat Mass Transf 147 (2020) 118889. bibhttps://doi.org/10.1016/j.ijheatmasstransfer.2019.118889.
7. G. Kailkhura, R. Mandel, A. Shooshtari, M. Ohadi, Experimental Study of a Set of Integrated Cross-Media Heat Exchangers (iCMHXs) for Liquid Cooling in Desktop Computers, ASME 2020 International Technical Conference and Exhibition on Packaging and Integration of Electronic and Photonic Microsystems (2020). bibhttps://doi.org/10.1115/IPACK2020-2591.
8. V. Ayyagari, G. Kailkhura, R. Mandel, A. Shooshtari, M. Ohadi, Performance Characterization of a Novel Low-Cost Additively Manufactured PCM-Air Polymer Composite Thermal Energy Storage, in: 2022 21st IEEE Intersociety Conference on Thermal and Thermomechanical Phenomena in Electronic Systems (ITherm), IEEE, 2022: pp. 1–9. bibhttps://doi.org/10.1109/iTherm54085.2022.9899596.
9. W. Ali, M. Echeverry-Rendón, A. Kopp, C. González, J. LLorca, Effect of surface modification on interfacial behavior in bioabsorbable magnesium wire reinforced poly-lactic acid polymer composites, Npj Mater Degrad 7 (2023) 65. bibhttps://doi.org/10.1038/s41529-023-0 0386-x.
10. L.P. Canal, C. González, J. Segurado, J. LLorca, Intraply fracture of fiber-reinforced composites: Microscopic mechanisms and modeling, Compos Sci Technol 72 (2012) 1223–1232. bibhttps://doi.org/10.1016/j.compscitech.2012.04.008.
11. P. Eyer, J. Dittus, A. Trauth, S. Coutandin, J. Fleischer, K.A. Weidenmann, Improvement of the adhesion in functional NiTi wire/polymer composites made by additive manufacturing, Compos Struct 275 (2021) 114455. bibhttps://doi.org/10.1016/j.compstruct.2021.114455.

Chapter 4
Accelerated Mechanical Behavior Characterization of Structural Materials

J. Rathore, A. Imeri, E. Al Amiri, V. Shah, C. O'Brien, B. Wisner, and A. Kontsos

Abstract Qualification processes for the mechanical behavior of advanced materials depend heavily on extensive experimental testing needed to also obtain inputs to both physics-based and machine learning models. The use of full-field methods has some inherent advantages towards the direction of accelerating such qualification compared with traditional mechanical testing approaches. To demonstrate an application of this potential, a novel specimen design is produced to obtain all input parameters to a J_3-type plasticity model that can characterize the plastic behavior of any type of alloy (in terms of crystallography), while also including the effects of anisotropy and strength differential dependencies. This work presents details on how Digital Image Correlation (DIC) could be used first to obtain mechanical behavior information from tests using standardized geometries which are then used to uniquely define input parameters for the plasticity model. This information is then leveraged to accelerate the plasticity model calibration process by using Finite Element Analysis (FEA) to design a novel test specimen geometry which can produce the same information by a 4-fold reduction of the associated number of experiments. Finally, this presentation concludes with the validation of the results obtained by the use of this novel specimen and by furthermore demonstrating how the FEA model could be used to augment the DIC information by computing the components of the strain tensor that are not measured by DIC while also providing the stress tensor components and related reaction forces.

Keywords Mechanical Testing · Digital Image Correlation · Plasticity

Introduction

Novel developments and performance improvement of advanced materials are hindered by the time involved between discovery and adoption. This is particularly true for the case of advanced manufacturing materials where small changes in the feedstock, process and post-process create unpredictable changes in the resulting mechanical behavior [1, 2]. Thorough understanding of material behavior requires exhaustive testing under various loading and environment conditions[3]. Additionally, testing is also used to develop and calibrate mathematical models (e.g. constitutive laws) to be used, for example, in Finite Element Analysis (FEA). Advanced materials used in engineering applications typically experience complex stress states which cannot be captured by simple specimen geometries, as defined e.g. by common standards[4]. In addition, most conventional and standardized testing methods use point-wise global measurements such as extensometers and strain gauges to provide bulk or global information (typically stress-strain curves). Furthermore, depending on the manufacturing methods used, materials can exhibit anisotropic, differential hardening, damage and other stress-state dependent effects (e.g. triaxiality), which cause non-homogenous stress and strain fields and add difficulty in developing reliable and accurate computational models.

J. Rathore · A. Imeri · E. Al Amiri · V. Shah · A. Kontsos(✉)
Digital Engineering Hub, Department of Mechanical Engineering, Henry M. Rowan College of Engineering, Rowan University, Glassboro, NJ 08028
email: rathor12@students.rowan.edu; imeri@rowan.edu; alamir78@rowan.edu; shahva28@rowan.edu; kontsos@rowan.edu

B. Wisner · C. O'Brien
Center for Advanced Materials Processing, Department of Mechanical Engineering Russ College of Engineering and Technology, Ohio University, Athens, OH 45701
email: bwisner@ohio.edu

Emily Retzlaff et al. (eds.), *Mechanics of Additive & Advanced Manufacturing, Inverse Methods and Machine Learning, Vol. 5*, Conference Proceedings of the Society for Experimental Mechanics Series, https://doi.org/10.13052/9788743808312-4

The emergence of non-contact optical methods such as Digital Image Correlation (DIC) has made it possible to perform full-field deformation measurements [5]. Since the 1980's DIC has been used extensively for evaluating mechanical properties of various materials at room temperatures and extreme conditions. The ability to analyze full-field measurements has the advantage of inspecting multi-stress modes present in a specimen or a part by probing specific regions of interest on the same field of view [6]. This capability has also allowed recently the design of unconventional specimen geometries that can imitate the complex loading modes found at the component level [6, 7]. This new approach of determining mechanical constitutive parameters has been coined as 'Material Testing 2.0' (MT2.0) by Pierron and Grediac [8]. Following this approach, several examples of novel specimens that capture more than one stress mode have been developed. For example, Khameneh et al. designed a specimen from which they examined the influence of tension regions and the geometry of shear region on the development of shear stress state in conjunction with FEA for fracture characterization of DP1180 steel [7]. Bensing et al. developed a specimen for evaluation of tensile and compression properties of thermoplastic polymers [6]. To further support the development of accelerated measurement of constitutive parameters, Jones et al. provided full-field DIC, and infrared thermography (IR) data tested at different rates and direction for seven unique geometries[9]. Multimodal stress state data becomes important in calibrating FEA models. For example, a general yield function developed by Lou et al. involves four stress modes analysis for computing hardening behavior that can exhibit differential and anisotropic hardening [10].

In this context, the research reported in this investigation presents an approach to design a specimen from which four independent stress states could be simultaneously activated at different regions and for the same load increment to allow measurements that provide the unknown coefficients of a J_3-plasticity type constitutive model developed by Lou et al. This manuscript is organized as follows: section 2 presents details on the J_3-plasticity model and the material information for the representative materials that the reported approach was applied. Section 3 provides details on the design of the complex shaped specimen. Section 4 shows validation efforts which included experiments in which DIC measurements and FEA results were used. The manuscript ends with concluding remarks on the overall usefulness of this approach and possible future steps.

Background

Plasticity model and Finite Element Analysis approach

In this research, we are using the model developed by Lou et al. [10] and which intends to capture both anisotropy and multiple stress-state dependence in the plastic behavior. The Lou model is a J_3 stress invariant type plasticity formulation, capable of describing the complex stress effects that could be present e.g., in metal forming. Equation 1 shows the definition of the yield surface for this model

$$f(\sigma_y) = a(\bar{\varepsilon}_p)\left\{b(\bar{\varepsilon}_p) I_1 + \left[\left(J_2^3 - c(\bar{\varepsilon}_p) J_3^2\right)^{1/2} - d(\bar{\varepsilon}_p) J_3\right]^{1/3}\right\} - \bar{\sigma}_{UT}(\bar{\varepsilon}_p) = 0, \quad (1)$$

where I_1 is a stress invariant of the Cauchy stress tensor, and J_2 and J_3 are the stress invariants of the deviatoric stress tensor. The parameters "a", "b", "c" and "d" that appear in Eq. (1) are determined using experimental data and the four equations summarized in Eq. (2)

$$\begin{cases} a = \frac{\sqrt{3}\bar{\sigma}_{UT}}{\bar{\sigma}_{SS}} \\ b = \frac{1}{3}\left(\frac{\bar{\sigma}_{SS}}{\bar{\sigma}_{PST}} - 1\right) \\ d = \frac{24}{7}\left[\left(\frac{\bar{\sigma}_{UT}}{a\bar{\sigma}_{UC}} + b\right)^3 - \left(\frac{1}{a} - b\right)^3\right] \\ c = \frac{1}{4}\left\{27 - \left[27\left(\frac{1}{a} - b\right)^3 + 2d\right]^2\right\} \end{cases} \quad (2)$$

where $\bar{\sigma}_{UT}, \bar{\sigma}_{SS}, \bar{\sigma}_{PST}$ and $\bar{\sigma}_{UC}$ are the von Mises equivalent stress at uniaxial tension, shear, plane strain tension and uniaxial compression states, respectively. Parameter "a" in the yield function provides scaling, "b" relates to pressure dependency, "c" defines curvature, and "d" is the strength differential. Based on different values of the hardening parameters and auto-differentiability the yield function can take the shape of yield surfaces such as von-Mises ($a = \sqrt{3}$, $b = 0, c = 0, d = 0$), Drucker Prager ($a, b, c, d = 0$), Cazacu Barlat ($a, b = 0, c = 0, d$) etc. Due to this ability of polymorphism, the Lou yield surface is considered as a robust candidate for mechanical behavior characterization. Figure 1 describes the triaxiality vs Lode mapping of the stress states required to calibrate the shape of the yield surface. The corresponding four types of specimen tests, i.e. dogbone (Uniaxial Tension - UT), notched tension (Plane Strain Tension), simple shear and cylinder

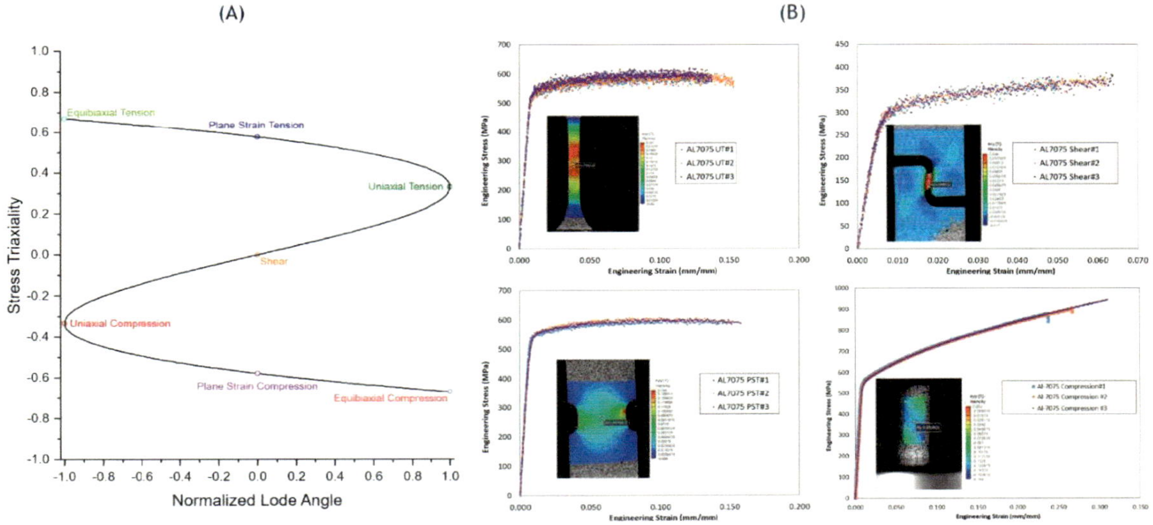

Fig. 1 (A) Lode vs Triaxiality visualization to define several stress states as proposed by Lou et al. [10]; (B) the 4 specimen geometries that correspond to 4 distinct stress states (per Eq. (2)), along with representative stress-strain and full-field metrology data obtained using the Digital Image Correlation (DIC) method

compression (Uniaxial Compression - UC) are required to determine the unknown parameters a, b, c and d , as a function of Equivalent Plastic Strain (EPS).

The implicit associated Lou model was successfully implemented in ABAQUS using a UMAT subroutine with C3D8 type brick elements to perform non-linear analysis of the combination of geometries and their boundary value problems as dictated by standard experimentation setups, procedures, and extracted calibration parameters.

Materials used and experimental setup

Experiments for the evaluation of strain hardening parameters and complex specimen design process were performed using commercial Al7075-T6 (procured from OnlineMetals). A servohydraulic frame (MTS 370 Landmark; 100 kN load capacity) was used to impose quasi-static loading conditions with a deformation rate of 0.5 mm/min applied to five individual stress state geometries including uniaxial tension, plane strain tension, shear, and cylinder and non-conventional compression specimens as shown in Figure 2 [11]. Flat specimen geometries were cut using a waterjet cutter from a 2 mm thick

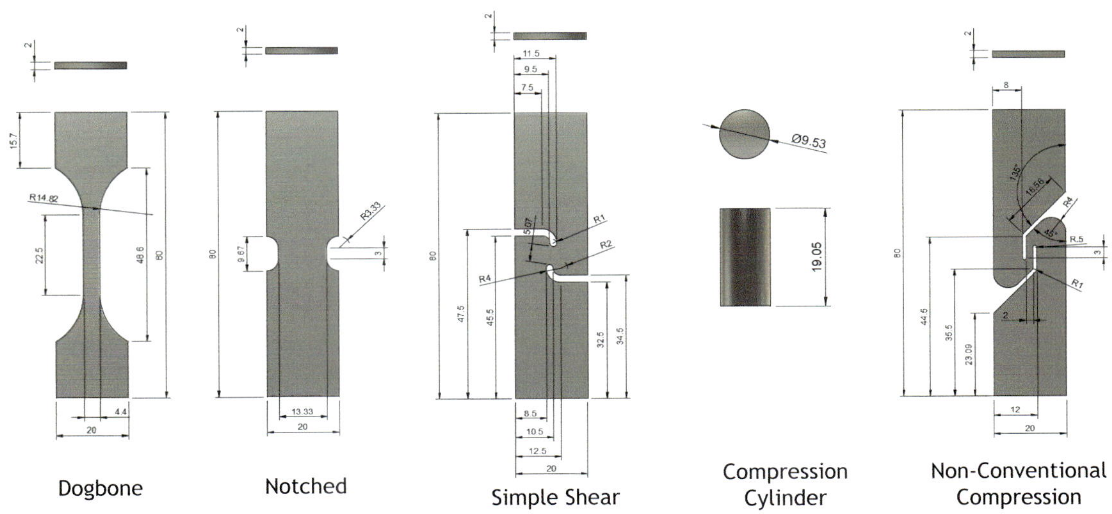

Fig. 2 Test specimen geometries used to obtain the stress-strain behavior of the Al7075-T6 material

sheet. For the compression cylinder specimens, a rod with a 9.525 mm diameter was cut with a 2:1 length-to-diameter ratio.

Full-field displacement and strain measurements were recorded using a stereo DIC system by Correlated Solutions as shown in Figure 3

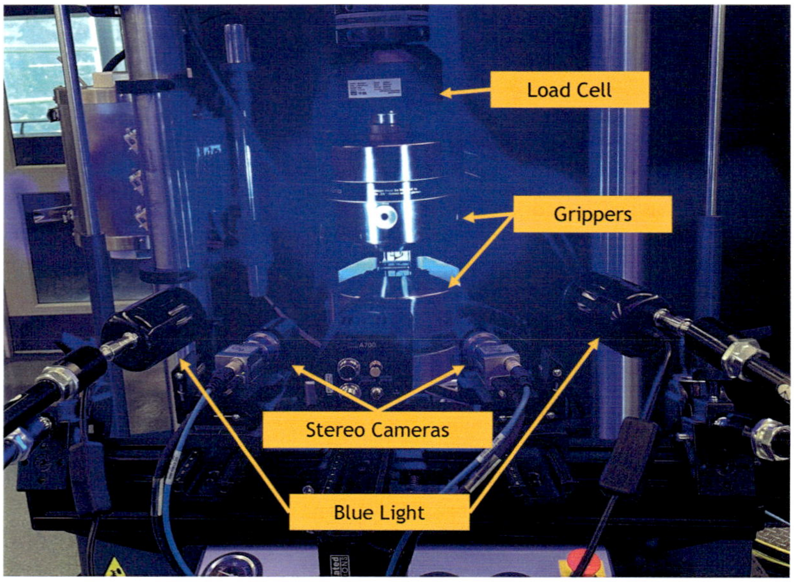

Fig. 3 Mechanical testing setup with DIC stereo system

Details about the testing machine and DIC system are shown in Table 1.

Table 1 Mechanical testing and DIC hardware and software parameters

Fixed Parameters		
	Machine Manufacturer & Model	MTS Landmark
	Grips	Flat wedge grips
	Load Cell	100 kN
	Displacement Rate	0.5 mm/min
	Data Acquisition Rate	100 Hz
DIC	Image Resolution	2448 × 2048 pixels
	Lens	Schneider f4.0/60 mm
	Image Acquisition Rate	2 Hz
	Patterning Technique	White & Black Spray Paint
	DIC Software	VIC 3D 10, Solution or system?
	Subset Weights	Gaussian
	Interpolant	Optimized 8-tap splines
	Strain Filter Window	15
	Strain Type	Hencky
	Calibration Grid	14 × 10 dots, 3 mm spacing

The DIC software parameters used are shown in Table 2. These parameters serve as quality control for the mechanical testing of each specimen. Additionally, for each test calibration, projection error, and noise floor measurements were recorded.

Table 2 An example of measured DIC parameters for a tested specimen

Parameters	Average
Noise Floor ($\mu\varepsilon$)	19.5
FOV ($\mathrm{mm} \times \mathrm{mm}$)	54×45
In-Plane Measurement Resolution (μm)	0.27
Subset & Step Size (px)	29×7
Projection Error (Avg)(< 0.1)	0.032
Calibration Score (< 0.1)	0.029
Magnification (px/mm)	45.58

The $\mathrm{a}, \mathrm{b}, \mathrm{c}, \mathrm{d}$ parameters determined for this material and used in this investigation are shown in Figure 4.

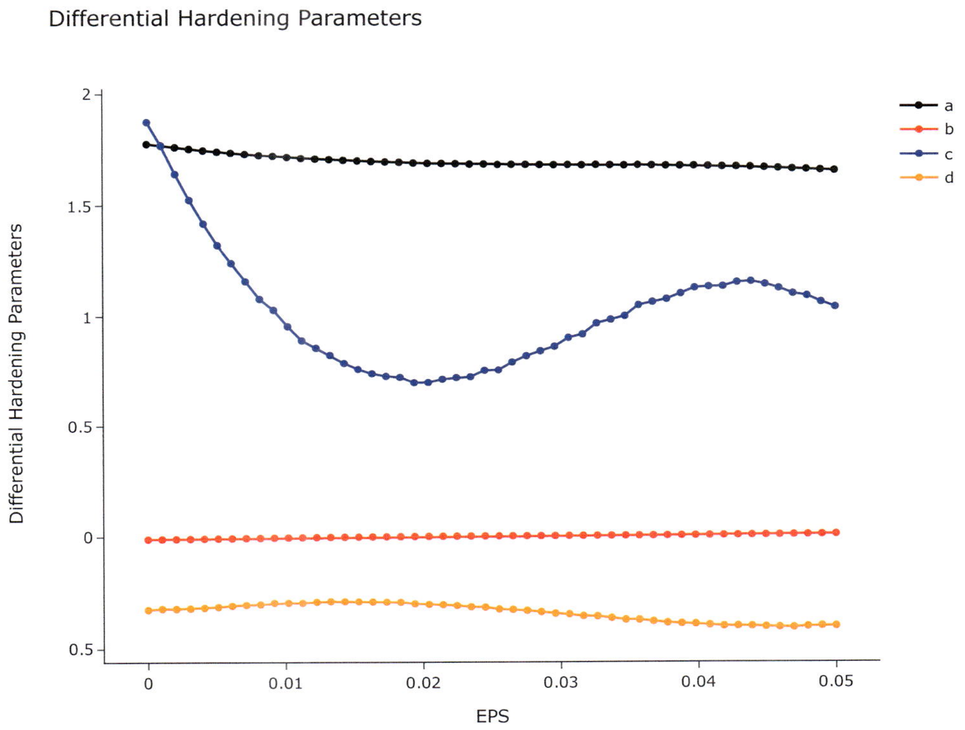

Fig. 4 Differential hardening parameters $\mathrm{a}, \mathrm{b}, \mathrm{c}$ and d for Lou model calibration

Analysis

Complex specimen design

In a multiple stress state specimen, Bensing et al. with the tension/compression and Khameneh et al. with the UT/shear specimen have shown the possibility of simultaneous stress state development on the same specimen [6, 7]. However, deformation associated with one stress state was found to have an adverse effect in localized property extraction such as modulus and poisson ratio, even in the elastic regime. To circumvent this, the following assumption was considered: the material behavior under loading is assumed to be scale independent which allows scaling of the specimen geometry. With this assumption, in elastoplastic materials such as metals, where the linear elastic deformation conforming to Hooke's Law is pronounced, the onset of plasticity at the yield point can be used to calibrate the combined geometry, as explained next.

In the case of combining two specimens such as standard tension and shear specimens, for a given elastoplastic material, experimental results show global loads F_1 and F_2 and overall displacements D_1 and D_2 at yielding, respectively. The geometries of tension and shear specimens can be then non-uniformly scaled such that:

$$F_1 = F_2 \tag{2}$$

$$D_1 = D_2 \tag{3}$$

This ensures simultaneous yielding as well as global load division by a factor (based on the assumed number of regions with independent stress states in the same specimen) to capture stress produced in each scaled specimen geometry.

In the case of a compression specimen, the load vector is in the opposite direction of tension, shear and notch tension specimens. Therefore, the M-specimen was utilized to produce localized compression while the overall geometry is in tension [11]. This special specimen is termed as non-conventional (NC) compression specimen in this work. The NC compression specimen was benchmarked with a standard compression cylinder, as shown in Figure 5 and it was found that the NC compression specimen can recover compression modulus, yield point, and hardening behavior. Since the yield point is used to calibrate the geometry of the combined specimen, the material behavior captured by NC compression specimen was assumed to be adequate for the goals of this investigation. With the reversal of the load vector of compression cylinder, equations Eqs. (3) and (4) extend as follows:

$$F_1 = F_2 = F_3 = F_4 = F_T \tag{4}$$

$$D_1 = D_2 = D_3 = D_4 = D_T \tag{5}$$

The load and displacement equilibration Figure 6–7 does not consider the moments produced by the shear and NCcompression specimen. Due to this, the design of the specimen needs to be such that the moments of these geometries cancel each other out. In the combination geometry, the shear and NC-compression are kept as the central specimens, while the tension and notched tension specimens are at the edges. Also, the NC-compression specimen is placed horizontally flipped as compared to shear specimen. The notches in the notched specimen are scaled uniformly to adhere to ASTM standard to develop plane strain tension stress state. The specimens in the combination geometry are given spaces on either side to allow horizontal deformations and prevent collisions. These steps are crucial to ensure the development of the stress state is similar to the development in individual standard specimens Figure 8.

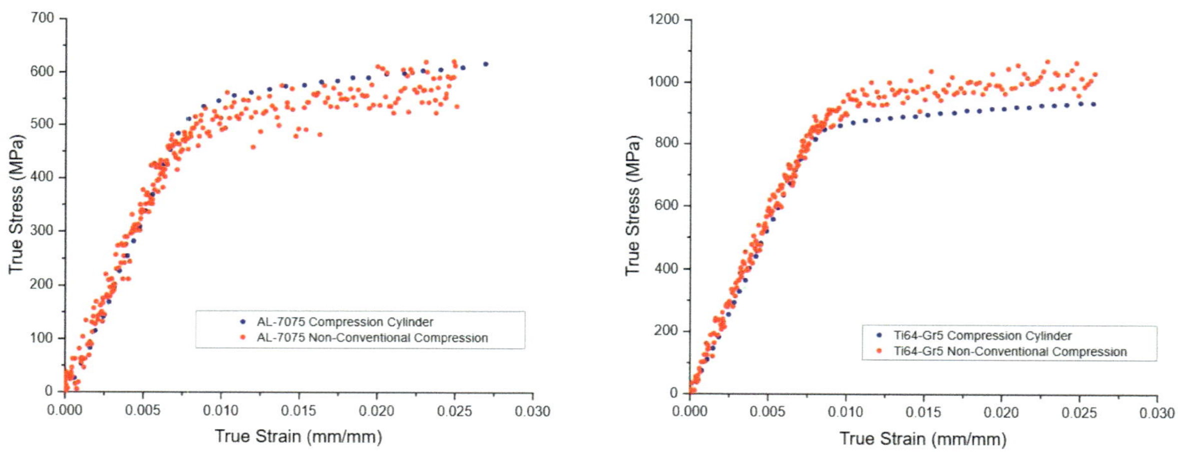

Fig. 5 Comparison of the behavior for the NC compression specimen with respect to ASTM E9 for two commercial materials

The target force parameter F_T and target displacement parameter D_T at yielding are calibrated using custom parametric modeling and are conformed to meet the manufacturing constraints of the gauge sections. For the case of A17075-T6, the F_T and D_T parameters are calibrated to be 2500 N and 0.45 mm respectively. The specimen is further scaled uniformly to fit a $40\ \mathrm{mm} \times 60\ \mathrm{mm}$ dimension to minimize material usage and maximize number of tests for a given volume of material (Figure 9). This specimen is termed as High Throughput (HTr) in the remainder of this manuscript.

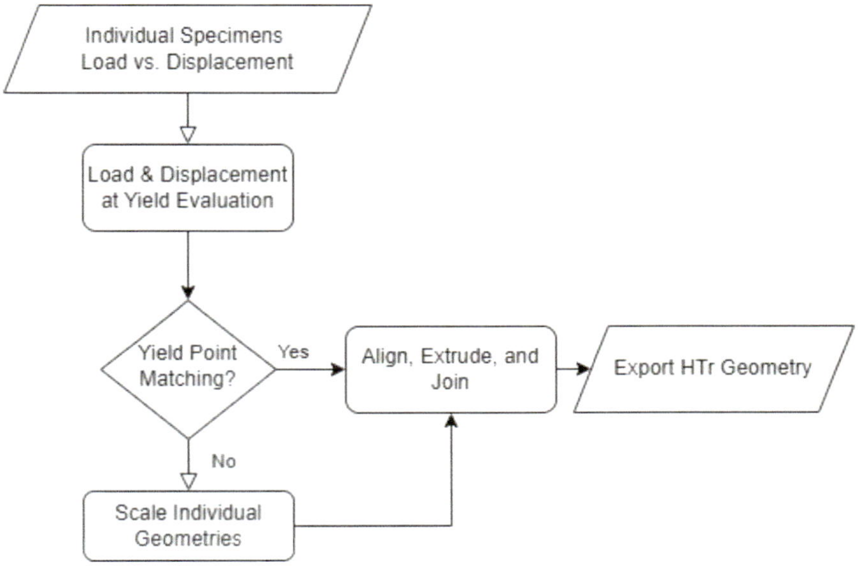

Fig. 6 Overall schematic of the design process for the HTr specimens for each unique material

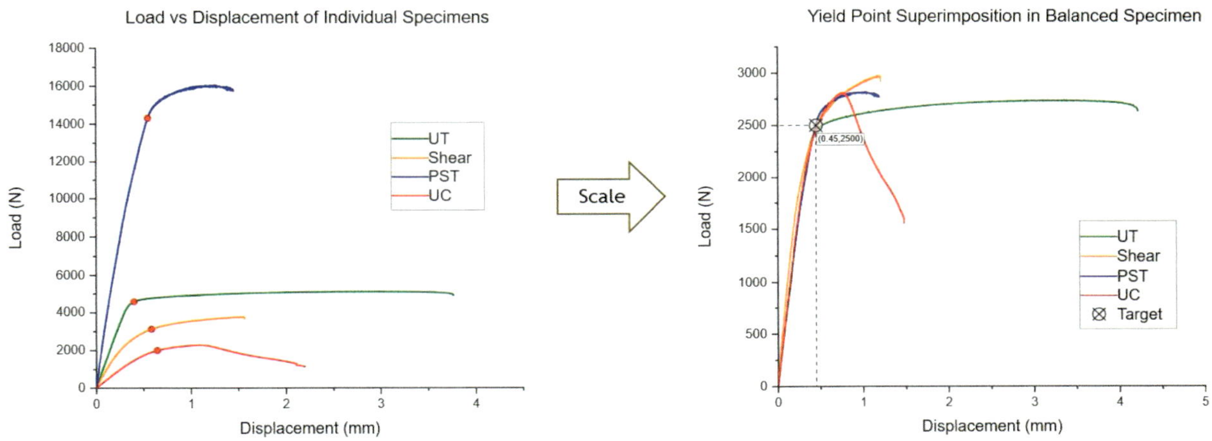

Fig. 7 Scaling of the load-displacement measurements for individual specimens to a common yield load and displacement

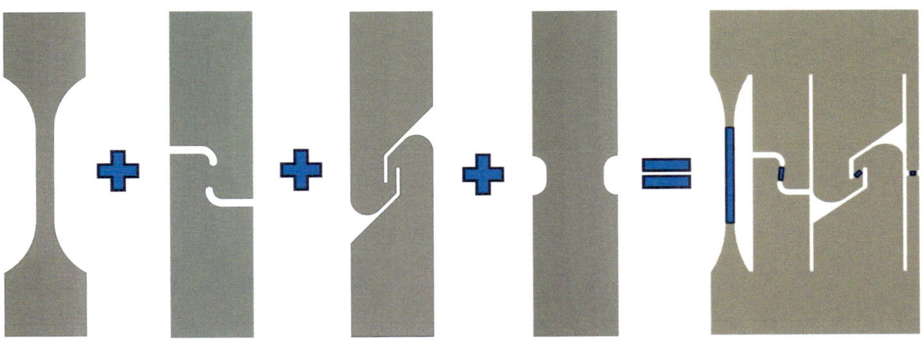

Fig. 8 Combination of the individual specimens to form the complex designed specimen

HTr is simulated with the rigid constraints on the gripping regions and a ramp displacement input at one gripping region while the other is fixed. The J_2 and Lou plasticity models were used in the simulation with the outputs being nodal

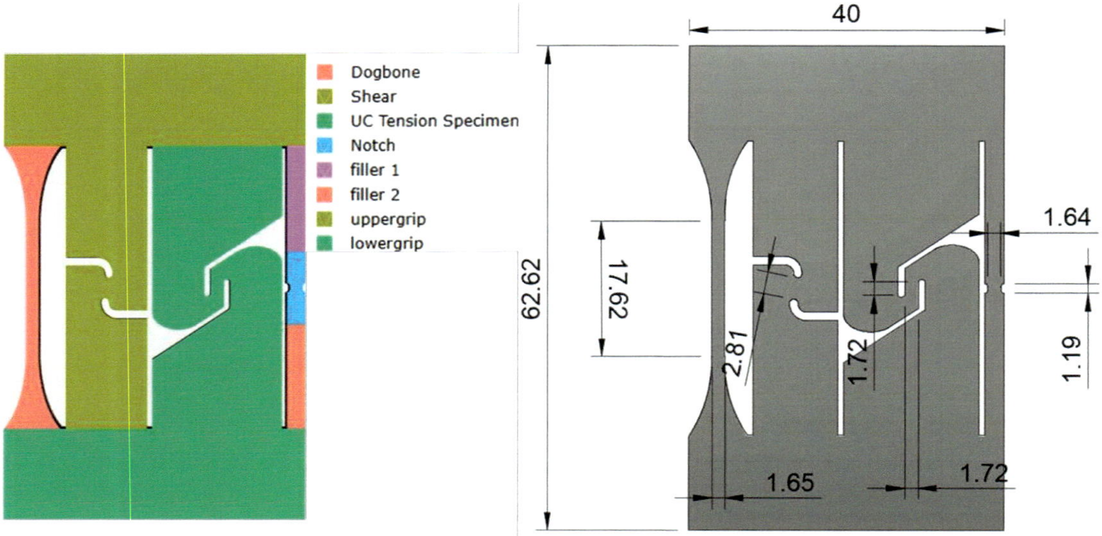

Fig. 9 Left: joining of the individual geometries with gripping and filling areas, right: the generated HTr specimen for a balanced yield load and displacement points for Al7075-T6

displacements, elemental stress and strain for each element as a field output, as well as the global reaction forces. The probing regions were detected using the Lode vs Triaxiality development of the elements in the gauge section of each specimen in HTr (Figure 10). The element groups that showed proper development of Lode and triaxiality for each stress state were combined to form regions of interest to be probed in FEA, as well as experimentation to extract data. From the region of interests in FEA, the average of strains and stresses is extracted as the local stress response for each stress state but also, the load derived stresses were determined using load division by 4 and then further divided by cross section area of each specimen in HTr to capture geometry induced effects. FEA provides the ability to decouple the geometry induced effects and plasticity model defined local response which provides further insight into the performance of the HTr specimen in terms of deviations for expected results.

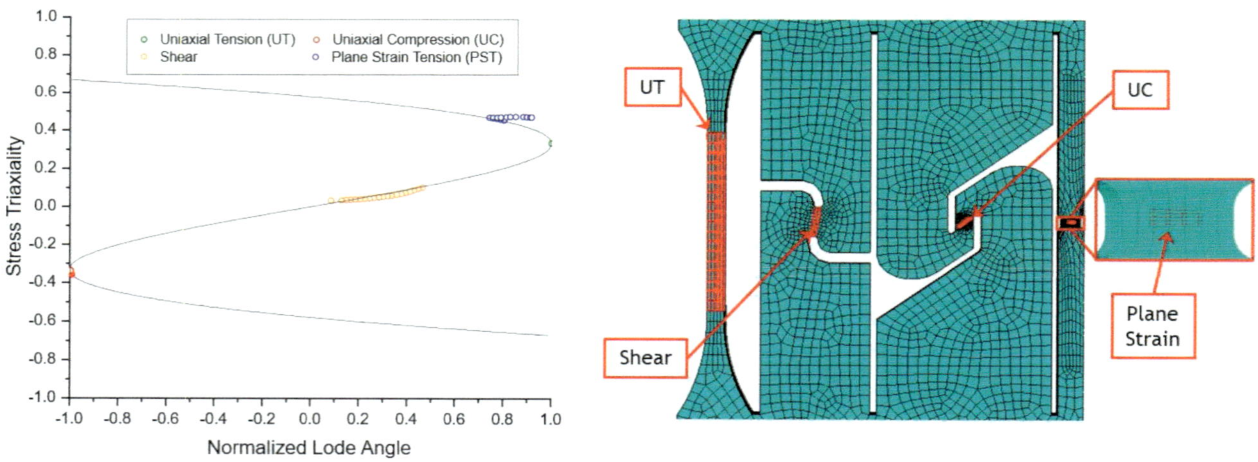

Fig. 10 Validation of the stress mode extracted from the HTr regions of interests (right) with the lode vs. triaxiality plot (right)

Validation

The HTr specimen was loaded experimentally in displacement control until failure. The DIC measurements provided displacement and strain fields as well as global load and displacement measurements. The FEA identified region of interests was utilized to capture the strain of the appropriate stress state. Then, the procedure of derived stresses was followed by utilizing global loads and dividing by 4 to capture the theoretical load experienced by each specimen in HTr specimen. To validate that the HTr specimen can be used to collect DIC data that meet the requirements of the selected J_2 and J_3 plasticity models several computational and experimental steps were taken and shown in the following figures. First, a direct comparison between the full-field strain measurements using DIC and the implemented subroutine of the FEA Lou et al. approach are shown in Figure 11. This shows that the developed FEA subroutine for the HTr specimen is capable of computing correctly all the regions of interest that correspond to the locations where mechanical data needs to be extracted per the J_3 model requirements.

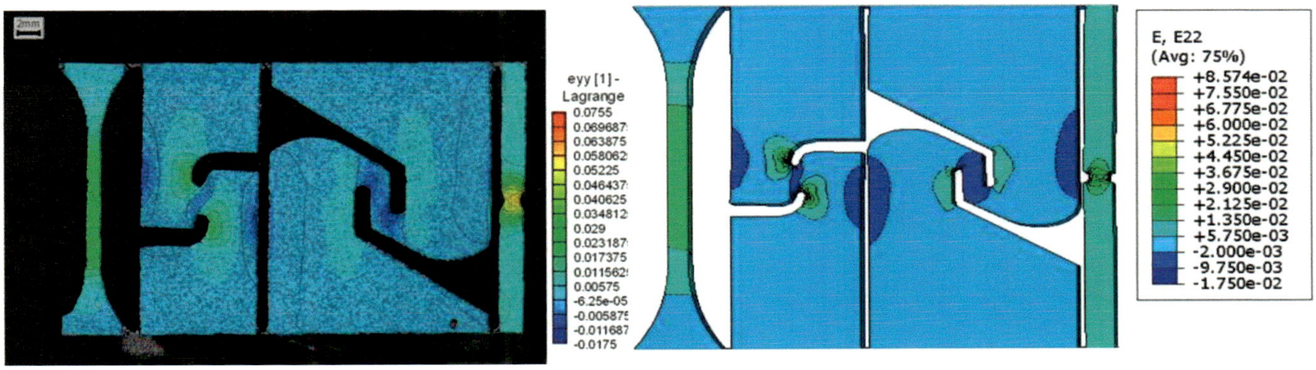

Fig. 11 Full-field strain DIC (left) and FEA(right) outputs scaled to similar contours

A direct comparison between HTr experiments with FEA results for all stress states is shown in Figure 12. The comparison demonstrates success in being capable of using a single complex to collect all data needed for the J_3 model. Additionally, direct comparison of the HTr collected experimental data with individual single stress mode data is shown in Figure 13. A good correlation between the obtained properties from both testing modes is observed.

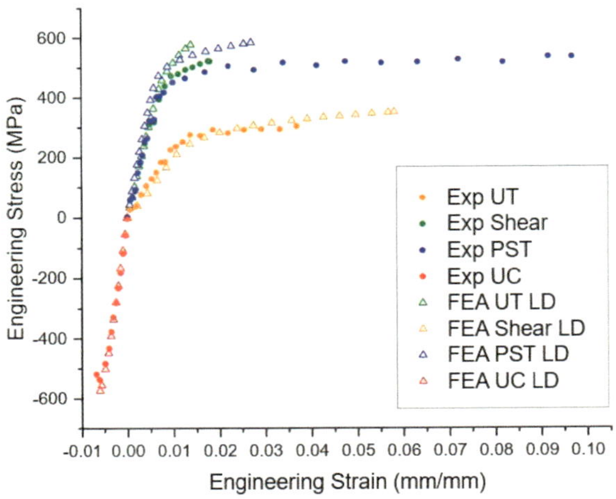

Fig. 12 Comparison of the engineering stress-strain behavior between the HTr experimental behavior to the FEA J_3HTr model

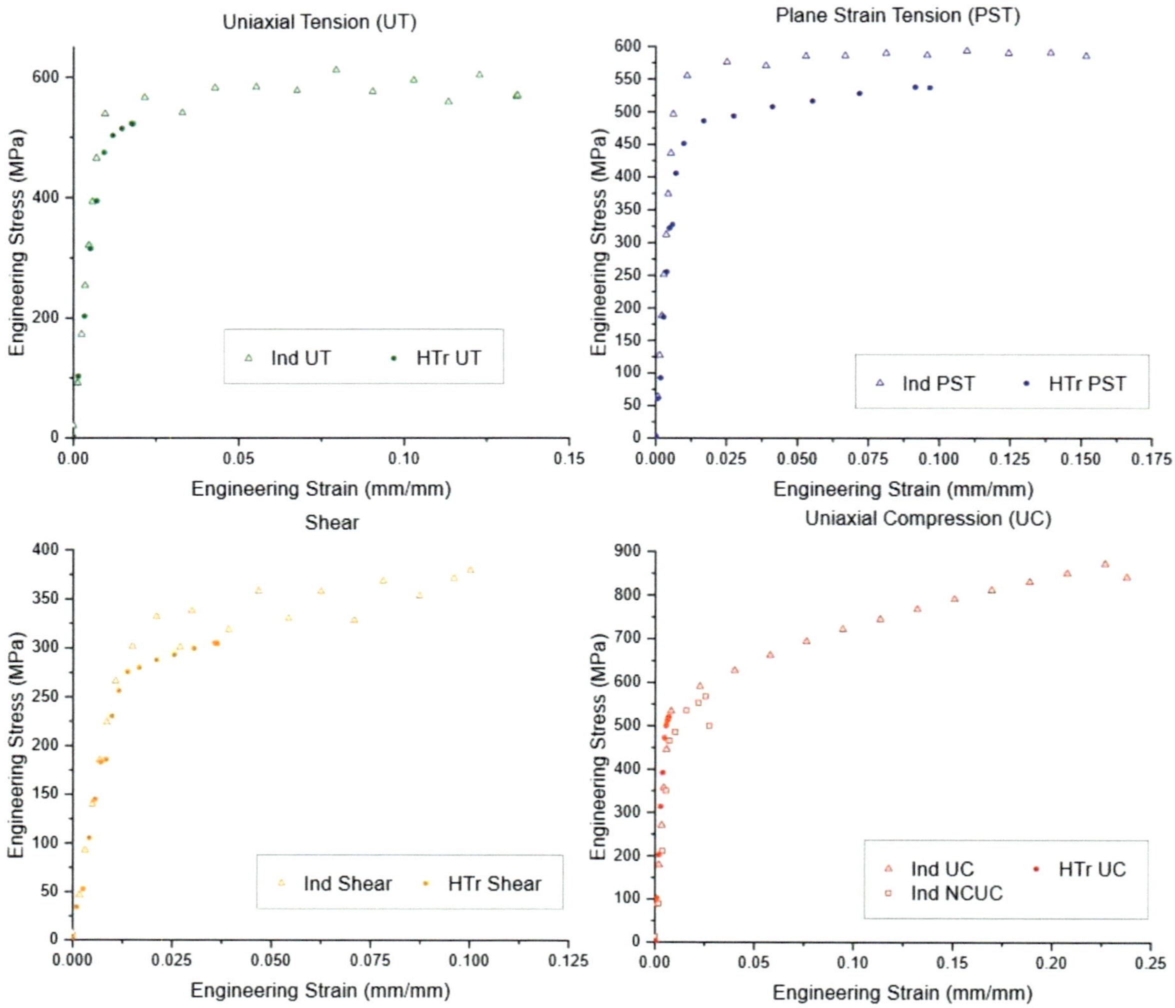

Fig. 13 Comparison of the stress-strain behavior between the individual and HTr specimens

Discussion

Utilizing the inherent advantages of the DIC displacement and strain measurements, the approach in this work showed that data that correspond to multiple stress modes can be extracted simultaneously. The proposed HTr specimen has been validated for commercial Al7075-T6 sheet with reliable results. Given four individual stress-strain cures, a unique for composition HTr can be generated and a J_3 plasticity model can then be calibrated. With the data availability of commercial materials, the experimental validation of FEA models can be reduced by a factor of four. If data is not available, at least one test per mode is still required, however, the repeatability of the behavior of the material can still be validated using the HTr specimen.

Concluding Remarks

In this study, an approach of designing a novel specimen was presented that could be used in tandem with a digital image correlation setup to obtain data corresponding to four stress modes needed to calibrate a J_3 plasticity model. Data from four individual specimens tested using conventional geometries, was used to generate this novel specimen and validation results were obtained to support this approach.

Acknowledgments The authors acknowledge the funding from the DARPA Multi-objective Engineering and Testing of Alloy Structures (METALS) research grant number HR001123S0029.

References

1. E. Tekerek et al., "On the process of designing material qualification type specimens manufactured using laser powder bed fusion," *Materials & Design,* vol. 229, p. 111893, 2023.
2. T. Kurzynowski, K. Gruber, W. Stopyra, B. Kuźnicka, and E. Chlebus, "Correlation between process parameters, microstructure and properties of 316 L stainless steel processed by selective laser melting," *Materials Science and Engineering: A,* vol. 718, pp. 64-73, 2018.
3. M. Rossi et al., "Testing methodologies for the calibration of advanced plasticity models for sheet metals: A review," *Strain,* vol. 58, no. 6, p. e12426, 2022.
4. B. Erice, C. C. Roth, and D. Mohr, "Stress-state and strain-rate dependent ductile fracture of dual and complex phase steel," *Mechanics of Materials,* vol. 116, pp. 11-32, 2018.
5. M. A. Sutton, J. J. Orteu, and H. Schreier, *Image correlation for shape, motion and deformation measurements: basic concepts, theory and applications.* Springer Science & Business Media, 2009.
6. T. Bensing and M. Moneke, "Development of a novel testing concept for combined characterisation of tensile and compressive properties," *International Journal of Mechanics and Materials in Design,* vol. 20, no. 5, pp. 895-907, 2024.
7. F. Khameneh, A. Abedini, and C. Butcher, "Experimental and Numerical Fracture Characterization of DP1180 Steel in Combined Simple Shear and Uniaxial Tension," *Metals,* vol. 13, no. 7, p. 1305, 2023.
8. F. Pierron and M. Grédiac, "Towards Material Testing 2.0. A review of test design for identification of constitutive parameters from full-field measurements," *Strain,* vol. 57, no. 1, p. e12370, 2021.
9. E. Jones et al., "Digital image correlation and infrared thermography data for seven unique geometries of 304L stainless steel," *Scientific Data,* vol. 11, no. 1, p. 1101, 2024.
10. Y. Lou, C. Zhang, S. Zhang, and J. W. Yoon, "A general yield function with differential and anisotropic hardening for strength modelling under various stress states with non-associated flow rule," *International Journal of Plasticity,* vol. 158, p. 103414, 2022.
11. D. Mohr and G. Gary, "M-shaped specimen for the high-strain rate tensile testing using a split Hopkinson pressure bar apparatus," *Experimental Mechanics,* vol. 47, pp. 681-692, 2007.

Chapter 5
Visco-plastic and Damage Characterization of Sheet Metals for Railway Crash Applications

Valentina Arrà, Mattia Utzeri, Gianluca Chiappini, Marco Sasso, and Alberto Perticone

Abstract This work investigates the visco-plastic behavior and damage evolution of stainless-steel sheet metals for railway crash applications under varying strain rates. The study combines quasi-static and dynamic tests, using a universal testing machine and a Split Hopkinson Bar (SHB), to evaluate the material response across a range of strain rates. The objective is to investigate how the yield surface evolves as a function of strain rate, evaluating the material's sensitivity to varying loading conditions. Additionally, the study aims to understand how these variations influence the failure strain and ductility, providing essential insights for enhancing the reliability of crashworthiness simulations.

To obtain a detailed description of the fracture locus, mechanical tests will be conducted on specimens with varying geometries, designed to induce both uniaxial and multiaxial loading conditions. This approach captures a wide range of stress states, enabling the calibration of the fracture locus as a function of triaxiality and Lode parameter to better understand how damage evolves under different strain rates.

Numerical simulations of the experiments were setup for calibration and validation purposes to ensure that the numerical models accurately represent the material behavior.

The plasticity model is identified using an inverse Finite Element (FE) approach, based on experimental data from both quasi-static and dynamic tests. The visco-plastic response of the sheet metals is then described using the Johnson-Cook and Cowper-Symonds models.

To replicate the damage initiation and progression, appropriate damage models are selected and implemented in ABAQUS FE software. The calibration process is based on a comparison between the simulated and experimental results, iteratively adjusting the model parameters until an optimal match is obtained. This iterative fitting allows for a comprehensive representation of the material behavior, capturing the influence of strain rate and stress state on the yield surface and fracture locus.

Keywords High strain rate · Hopkinson Bar · Stress Triaxiality · Ductile damage

Introduction

This study focuses on the mechanical characterization of 550W steel through static and dynamic tests, integrated with FEM simulations using Abaqus/CAE. The main objective is to calibrate a ductile damage model to predict material failure based on triaxiality and strain rate.

The importance of this research lies in the potential to improve the performance of structural materials used in high-stress applications, such as energy absorption systems for railway carriages [1, 2], by optimizing component safety and durability.

Valentina Arrà · Mattia Utzeri · Marco Sasso
Department of Industrial Engineering and Mathematical SciencesUniversità Politecnica delle Marche, 60131, Ancona - Italy
e-mail: v.arra@pm.univpm.it; m.utzeri@staff.univpm.it; m.sasso@univpm.it

Gianluca Chiappini
Università Telematica eCampusNovedrate, Como, 22060 – Italy
e-mail: g.chiappini@staff.univpm.it

Alberto Perticone
Hitachi Rail STS SpaCiliegiole, 51100 Pistoia – Italy
e-mail: alberto.perticone.ayes@hitachirail.com

Emily Retzlaff et al. (eds.), *Mechanics of Additive & Advanced Manufacturing, Inverse Methods and Machine Learning, Vol. 5*,
Conference Proceedings of the Society for Experimental Mechanics Series, https://doi.org/10.13052/9788743808312-5

Understanding the mechanical behavior of 550W steel fits into a broader context of studies analyzing the relationship between triaxiality and ductile fracture. Models like Rice-Tracey [3], Hancock-Mackenzie [3] and Bao-Wierzbicki [5] have highlighted the correlation of ductility with stress triaxiality. Bai-Wierzbicki [6] and Dunand-Mohr [7] studied the effect of Lode angle. Since the seminal work of Johnson-Cook [8], another important parameter is known to be represented by strain rate, where triaxiality and strain rates are considered in an uncoupled way; several damage models account for such parameters thus describing a fracture locus or fracture surface as a function of Lode angle, triaxiality and strain rate [9]. Further works included the temperature effect, both in terms of initial temperature and self-heating due to plastic work [10].

This research adopts a mixed experimental-numerical approach, calibrating the Bao-Wierzbicki [5] model based on collected experimental data and validated through FEM simulations. Differently from Johnson-Cook model [8], the effect of strain rate will be considered with a non-monotonous polynomial law.

Methodology

The experimental tests were conducted on specimens of various geometries to achieve different stress states. The methodology involves five phases: i) specimen preparation, ii) test execution, iii) data acquisition and post-processing, iv) visco-plastic modeling, v) damage modeling. Four specimen geometries, shown in Figure 1, were extracted by laser cutting from 4 mm thick plates of 550 weathering steel, to be tested with strain rates ranging from 10^{-2} to 10^{3} s^{-1}, [5].

The experimental tests were executed by an electro-mechanical testing machine (Zwick-Roell® Z050) and by a direct tension split Hopkinson Bar [12], capable of reaching strain rates up to 1000 s^{-1}. During the tests, key parameters like deformation, load, and failure mode were monitored using strain gauges and Digital Image Correlation (DIC) techniques. In

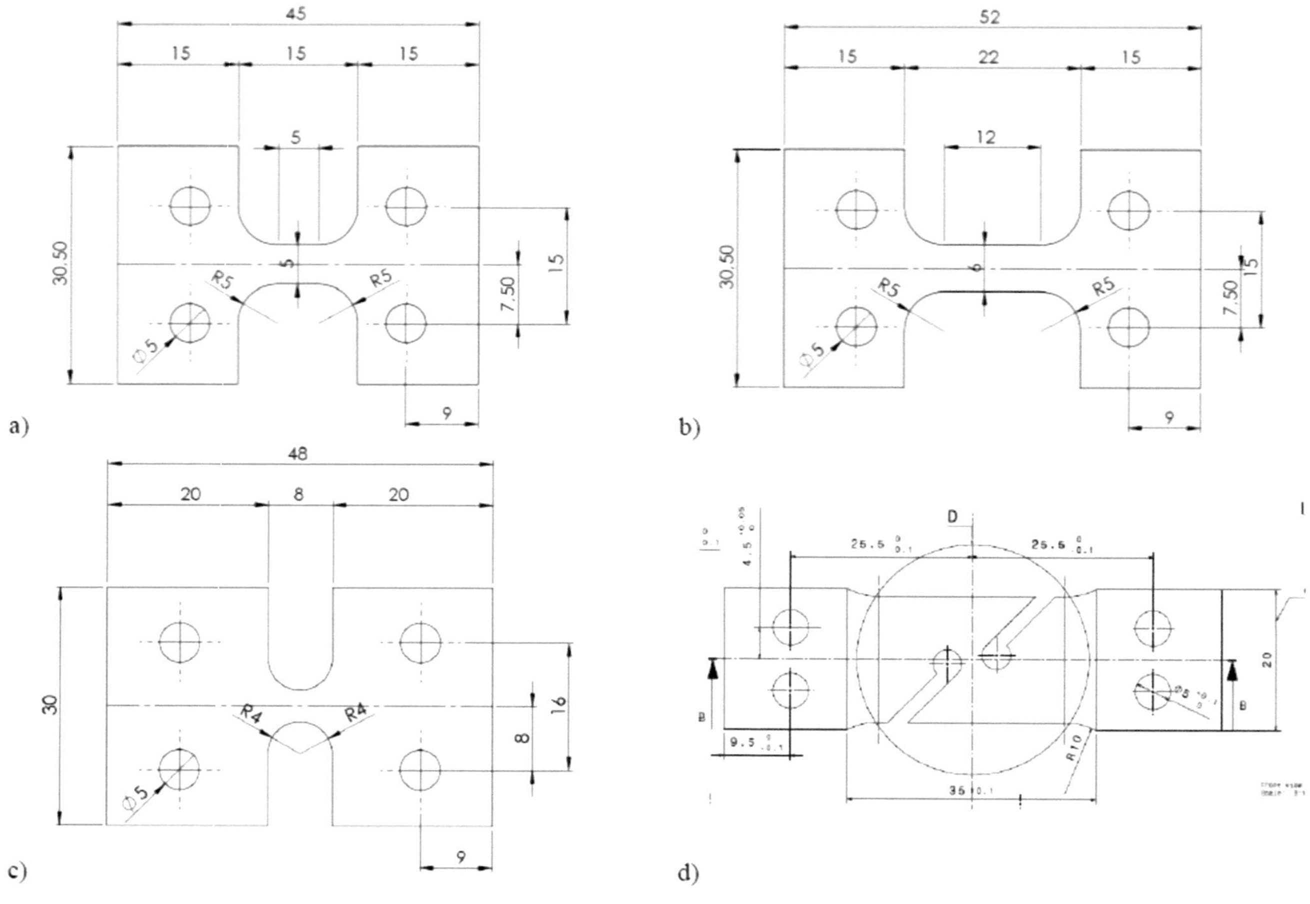

Fig. 1 Geometries of tested sample; a,b) P1 and P2 geometries for uniaxial tests at intermediate triaxiality; c) P3 notched geometry for high triaxiality; d) D10 Driemeier geometry [11] for low triaxiality testsbroken

particular, engineering uniaxial stress-strain curves were obtained for different strain rates using the P1 and P2 geometries; then, the average strain computed in the necking section from DIC analyses was used to convert the engineering data into first-attempt true stress-strain curves. A mixed analytical-numerical procedure was implemented: FEM simulations were repeated varying material parameters according to an optimization scheme, where deviations between numerical and experimental load-displacement curves are minimized. Figure 2 shows the 3D meshed models developed in Abaqus/Explicit ® software; the mesh size of all models was 0.25mm in the gauge area.

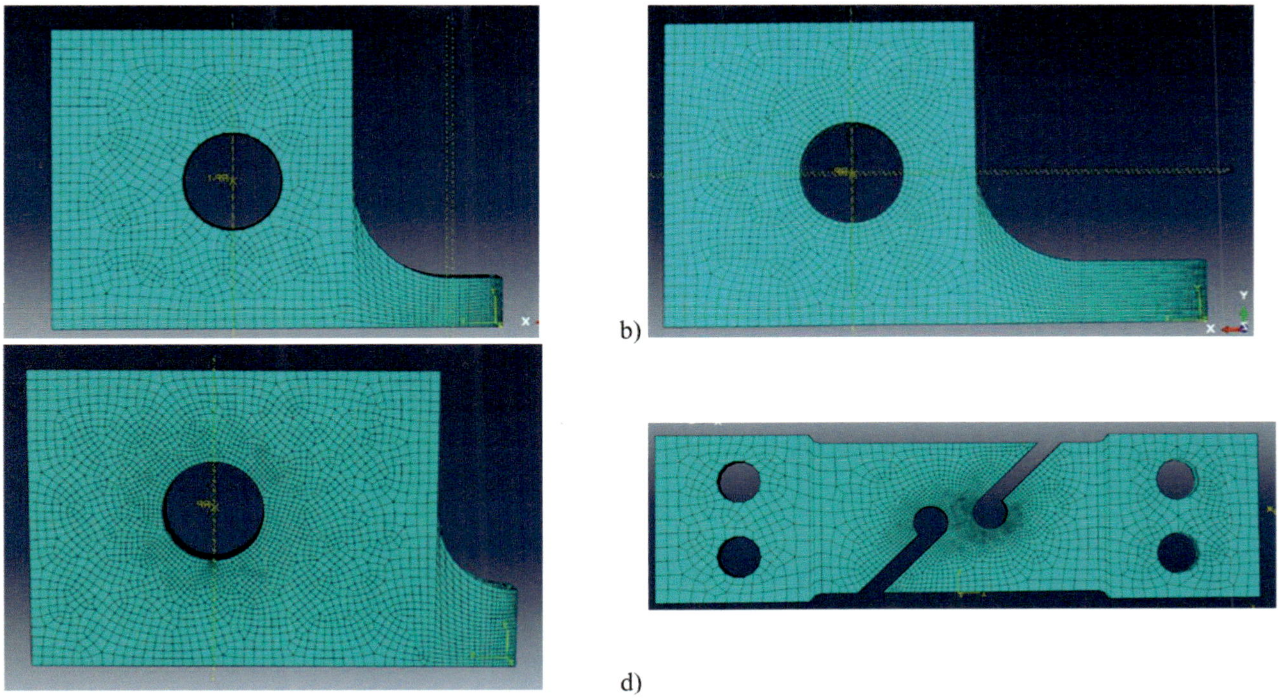

a) b) c) d)

Fig. 2 FE models in Abaqus/Explicit; a) P1 geometry, b) P2 geometry, c) P3 notched geometry, d) D10 geometry

The adopted visco-plastic law is given by the Voce's hardening law, combined with the Johnson-Cook strain rate dependency term [13], which was input in tabular form as material mechanical properties. The equation is:

$$\sigma = \{\sigma_0 + R_0 \cdot \varepsilon_{pl} + R_\infty \left[1 - exp\left(-b \cdot \varepsilon_{pl}\right)\right]\} \cdot \left[1 + q \cdot ln\left(\dot{\varepsilon}/\dot{\varepsilon}_0\right)\right] \tag{1}$$

After the visco-plastic model was calibrated, the same simulations were used to extract the characteristic parameters such as stress triaxiality and effective strain rate at the core of the samples; these data were used for the definition of a fracture locus in the (T, $\dot{\varepsilon}$, ε_f) space; in particular, the Bao-Wierzbicki model was first calibrated based on quasi-static results. The equation is divided into three regions, the first corresponding to shear cracking, the third to void growth, and the second corresponding to a mixed failure mode:

$$\begin{cases} region\ I: \ \varepsilon_f = a(T + 1/3)^b \\ region\ II: \ \varepsilon_f = cT^2 + dT + e \\ region\ III: \ \varepsilon_f = fT^{-1} \end{cases} \tag{2}$$

Then, the strain rate dependency was considered by a polynomial law of second and third-order, thus to define a 3D fracture surface:

$$f(T, \log(\dot{\varepsilon})) = c_1 + c_2 T + c_3 \log(\dot{\varepsilon}) + c_4 T^2 + c_5 T \log(\dot{\varepsilon}) + c_6 \log(\dot{\varepsilon})^2 \tag{3a}$$

$$f(T, \log(\dot{\varepsilon})) = c_1 + c_2 T + c_3 \log(\dot{\varepsilon}) + c_4 T^2 + c_5 T \log(\dot{\varepsilon}) + c_6 \log(\dot{\varepsilon})^2 + c_7 T^3 + c_8 T^2 \log(\dot{\varepsilon}) + c_9 T \log(\dot{\varepsilon})^2 + c_{10} \log(\dot{\varepsilon})^3 \tag{3b}$$

The coefficients were found by minimizing the distance between the points and the surface.

Results

The engineering curves of uniaxial tests at different strain rates on P1 and P2 samples are shown in Figure 3. The ductility of the material, in terms of strain to failure, is observed to be constant between quasi-static and intermediate strain rate; at higher strain rates, the ductility was found to decrease at approximately 500 s^{-1}, whereas it increases nearly to the quasi-static values at 1000 s^{-1}.

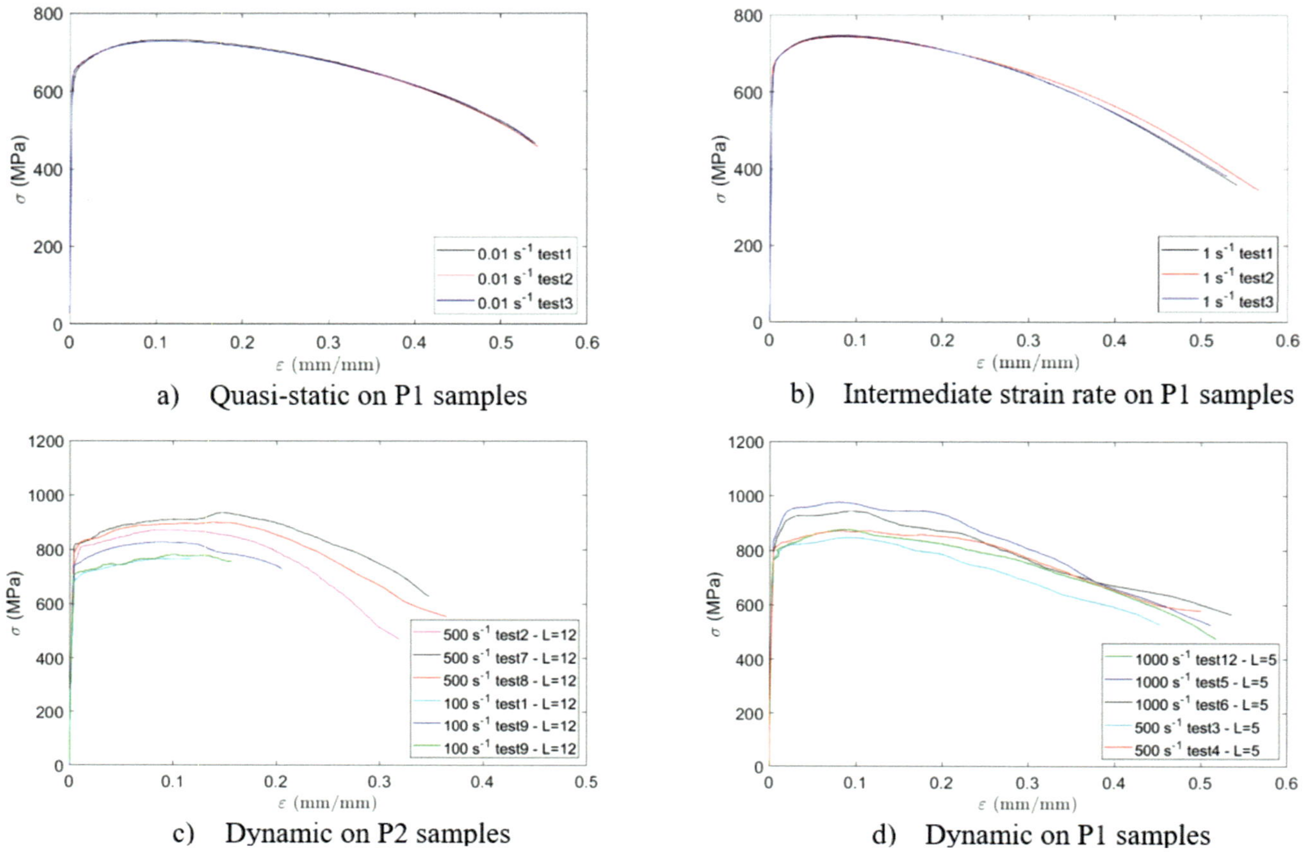

Fig. 3 FE models in Abaqus/Explicit; a) P1 geometry, b) P2 geometry, c) P3 notched geometry, d) D10 geometry

The results of uniaxial tests at different strain rates revealed that the strain rate dependence is indeed well described by a polyline with double slope in the double-logarithmic plane, as shown in Figure 4. It is noted that the strain rate affected material behavior mainly above a threshold strain rate $[\dot{\varepsilon_0}]$ of 155 s^{-1}. The parameters of the Voce's hardening law are reported in Table 1. The global material behavior was input as a tabular material card into Abaqus material properties.

Table 1 Voce's hardening parameters

σ_0 [MPa]	R_0 [MPa]	R_∞ [MPa]	b
644	260	226	7.63

Considering the visco-plastic behavior of the material, the numerical simulations showed a very good agreement with experimental data, in terms of reconstructed load-displacement curves, with deviations as low as 2.5%. Figures 5 show the curves of the P1 geometries tested at different strain rates. A similar agreement, not reported here for the sake of brevity, was found for the P3 Notched and D10 geometries.

After having validated the behavior of visco-plastic constitutive model, attention was paid to the deformation at failure. The average stress triaxiality and the equivalent plastic strain at the instant of failure was computed in the most critical elements of each model. The P1 and P2 samples showed the highest plastic strain at failure at the core elements. Notched specimens exhibited localized deformation concentrations in the notched area, with a reduced strain to failure, confirming the

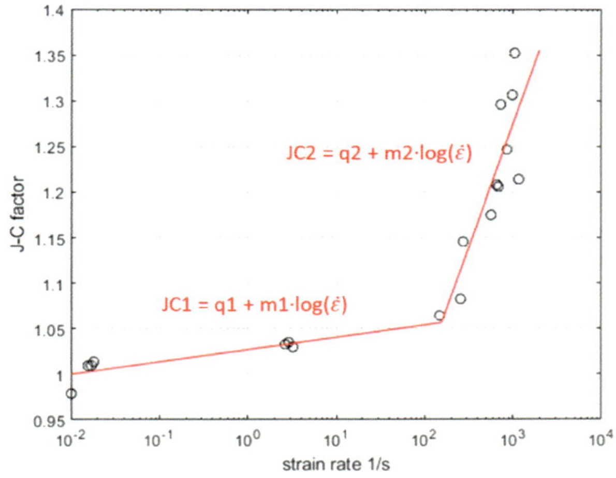

Fig. 4 strain rate dependency of material strength

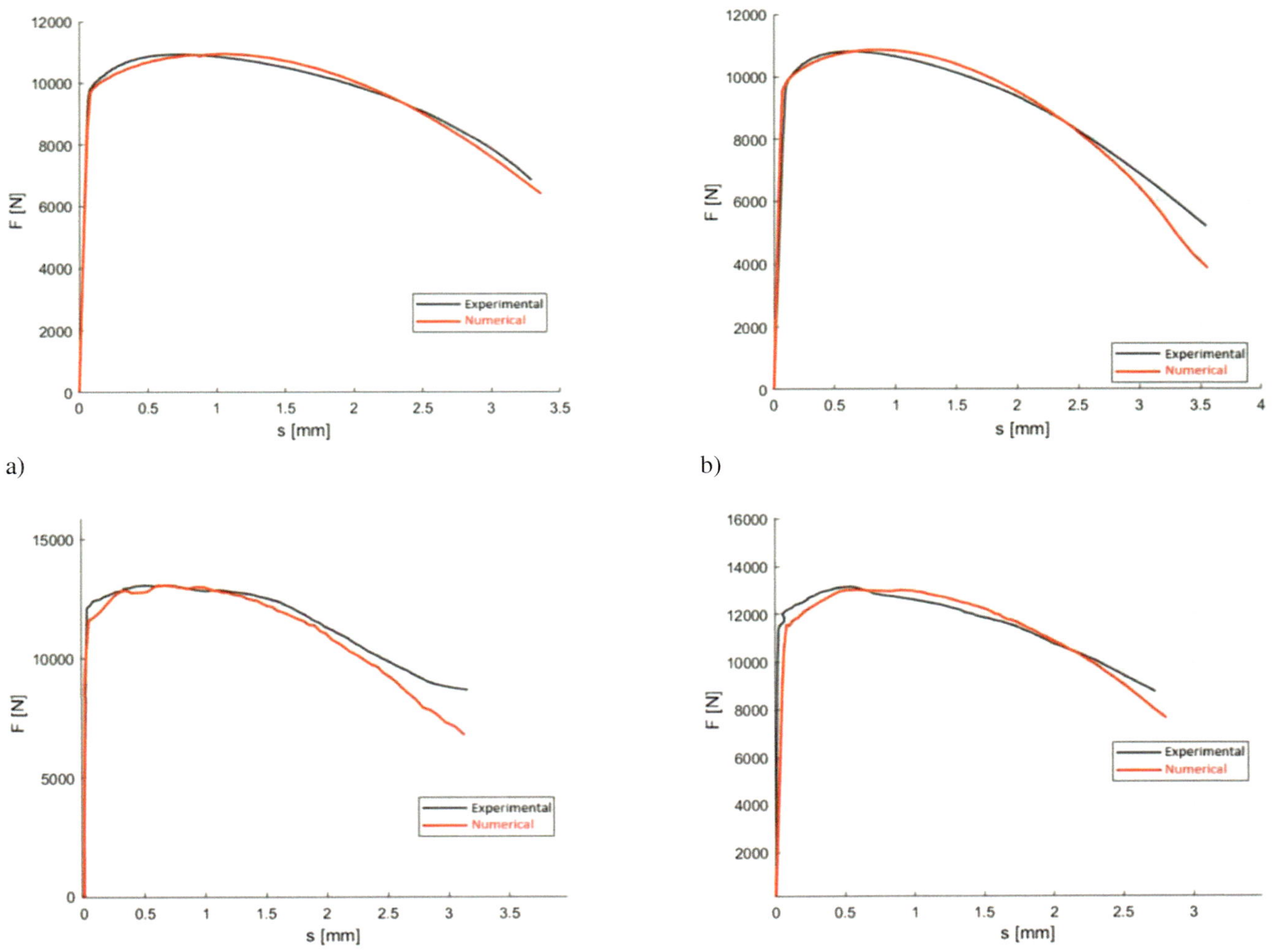

a)

b)

c)

d)

Fig. 5 Comparison of experimental and numerically reconstructed load-displacement curves for tests on P1 samples at different strain rates; a) 10^{-2} s^{-1}; b) 10^{0} s^{-1}; c) $5{\cdot}10^{2}$ s^{-1}; d) $10^{3}s^{-1}$

correlation between triaxiality and fracture behavior. Dremeier specimen revealed a strain to failure slightly lower than P1 and P2. Consequently, the comparison between the results obtained with empirical ductile damage models showed that the Bao-Wierzbicki model better represents the material's behavior compared to the Rice-Tracey or Cockcroft-Latham models. Figure 6a shows the trend of strain to failure as a function of stress triaxiality T in quasi-static conditions. The extension to strain rate as a third axis leads to the bi-cubic surface given in Figure 6b.

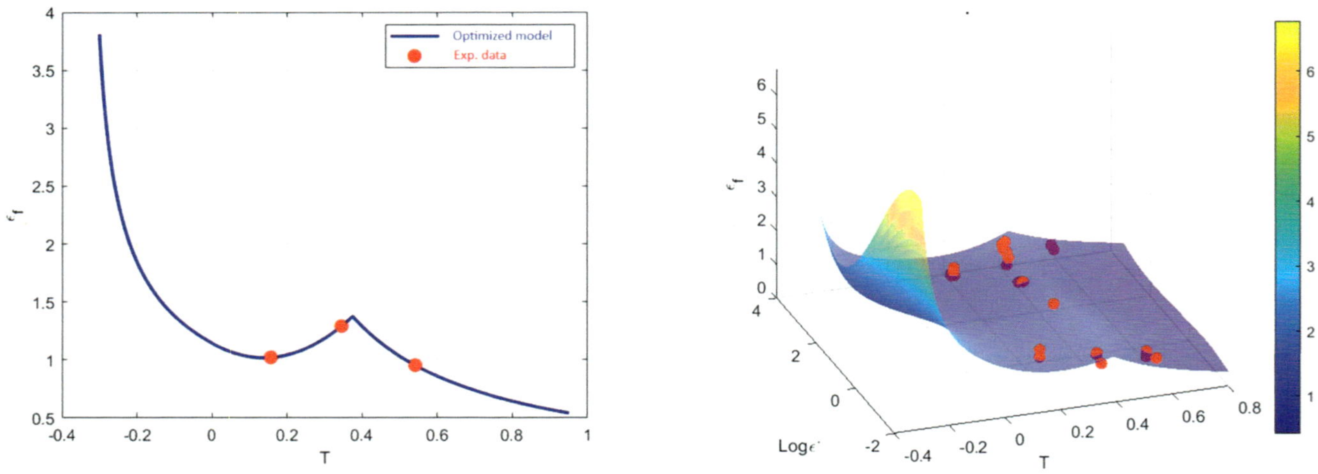

a) b)

Fig. 6 Calibrated Bao-Wierzbicki: a) application to quasi-static data; b) extension to strain rate effect by polynomial surface

The results demonstrate the validity of the chosen approach to describe the behavior of 550W steel under dynamic loads. The FEM methodology enabled the investigation of phenomena that are not directly measurable in the laboratory, such as the evolution of strain and stress tensors and the fracture surface. The Bao-Wierzbicki damage model showed high predictive capability for fracture in complex loading states. Nevertheless, Figures 7 show that the trend of the material ductility with strain rate is not very smooth; as a result, the simple quadratic law appears to be not well representative, whereas the cubic law is affected by a certain overfitting effect; further investigation is needed, especially at an intermediate strain rate.

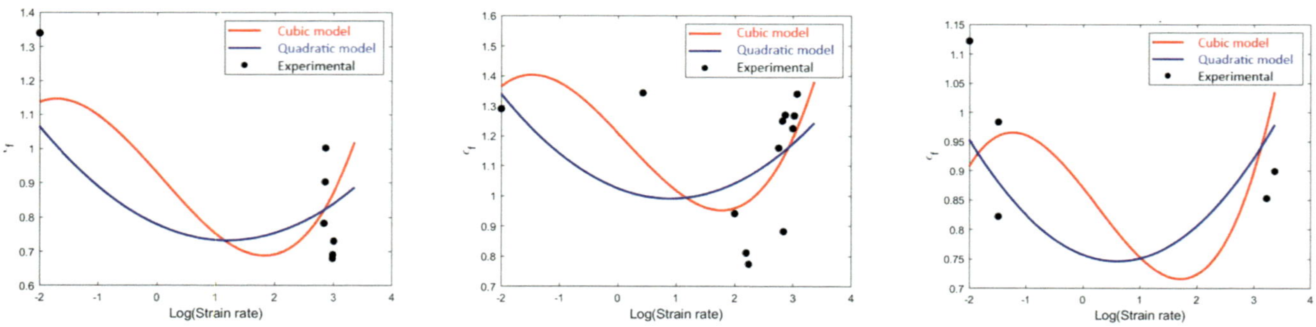

a) b) c)

Fig. 7 Trend of strain to failure at different strain rates and triaxiality values according to quadratic or cubic surface fitting: a) T = 0.14 (Driemeier samples), b) T = 0.34 (P1 and P2 samples), c) T = 0.54 (P3 notched samples)

Conclusion

The research confirms the reliability of the adopted approach in predicting the behavior of 550W steel under operational conditions and provides a significant contribution to the modeling of ductile damage in structural materials. The methodology adopted allowed for an accurate description of the material's behavior and successful calibration of the Bao-Wierzbicki damage model. The results can be applied to the railway industry to improve the performance of crash absorbers.

Future perspectives include the extension of tests to intermediate strain rates, and the implementation of an advanced damage model to account for varying strain rates with a more complex behavior rather than the simple quadratic or cubic law here adopted.

Acknowledgments The authors would like to express their gratitude to Hitachi Rail STA S.p.A., Ciliegiole, 51100 Pistoia – Italy for commissioning and supporting this research work. In particular, we thank them for providing the material, and for their valuable collaboration and scientific contributions during the various phases of the project.

References

1. Seung, R.K., and Jeong S.K., (2008) A study on strain rate effect in collision analysis of rolling stock, International Journal of Modern Physics B, 22:09n11, 1423-1430
2. Xie S., Du X., Zhou H., Wang D., Feng Z., (2020) Analysis of the crashworthiness design and collision dynamics of a subway train. Proceedings of the Institution of Mechanical Engineers, Part F: Journal of Rail and Rapid Transit 234(10):1117
3. Rice, J.R. and Tracey, D.M. (1969). On the ductile enlargement of voids in triaxial stress fields. Journal of the Mechanics and Physics of Solids.
4. Hancock J.W., and Mackenzie A.C., (1976). On the mechanisms of ductile failure in high-strength steels subjected to multi-axial stress-states. Journal of the Mechanics and Physics of Solids 24: 147–160
5. Bao, Y., and Wierzbicki, T. (2004). A Comparative Study on Fracture Models for Ductile Metals. International Journal of Mechanical Sciences.
6. Bai, Y., and Wierzbicki T (2008). A new model of metal plasticity and fracture with pressure and Lode dependence. International Journal of Plasticity 24: 1071–1096.
7. Dunand, M., and Mohr, D., (2011). On the predictive capabilities of the shear modified Gurson and the modified Mohr-Coulomb fracture models over a wide range of stress triaxialities and Lode angle. Journal of the Mechanics and Physics of Solids 59: 1374–1394.
8. Johnson, G.R. and Cook, W.H. (1985). Fracture characteristics of three metals subjected to various strains, strain rates, temperatures and pressures. Engineering Fracture Mechanics, 21:31–48.
9. Cortese L., Coppola T., Campanelli F., Campana F., and Sasso M., (2013). Prediction of ductile failure in materials for onshore and offshore pipeline applications, International Journal of Damage Mechanics, 23(1): 104-123
10. Cortis, G., Nalli, F., Sasso, M., Cortese, L., and Mancini, E., (2022). Effects of Temperature and Strain Rate on the Ductility of an API X65 Grade Steel, Applied Sciences Volume 12(5):2444
11. Brünig M, Chyra O, Albrecht D, Driemeier L., and Alves M. (2008). A ductile damage criterion at various stress triaxialities International Journal of Plasticity (24) 1731-55
12. Mancini, E.; Sasso, M.; Rossi, M.; Chiappini, G.; Newaz, G.; Amodio D., (2015). Design of an Innovative System for Wave Generation in Direct Tension–Compression Split Hopkinson Bar. J. Dyn. Behav. Mater. (1) 201–213
13. Johnson, G.R., and Cook, W.H. (1983). A constitutive model and data for metals subjected to large strains, high strain rates and high temperatures, Proceedings of the 7th International Symposium of Ballistics.

Chapter 6
Design and Optimization of Shock Absorbers Made of Grade Density Foams

C. Sabbatini, G. Zandri, and M. Sasso

Abstract In this paper, the adoption of density graded polymeric foams is evaluated for energy absorption purposes. The use of functionally graded materials is becoming increasingly widespread in the field of personal protection and industrial applications, thanks in part to recent advances that have simplified their production. To properly design an energy absorber, it is first necessary to identify the material used and characterize its behavior at different densities and strain rates. The necessary experimental tests were conducted using a pneumatic compression machine for low and intermediate strain rates, while for dynamic tests, the Hopkinson bar was employed. Tests were initially conducted on uniform samples of different densities; this allowed the analysis and calibration of a visco-elasto-plastic constitutive model borrowed from the literature. Then, the mentioned constitutive models have been implemented in numerical simulations with Abaqus/explicit finite element software, where the energy absorption capability of a density graded absorber was evaluated reproducing a puncture test. The density distribution in the absorber was designed and optimized to simultaneously reduce the peak of acceleration of the impacting mass and the maximum stress experienced by the absorber during the impact event.

Keywords Polymeric foams · Ogden hyperfoam model · Viscoelasticity · Functionally graded materials

Introduction

Polyvinyl chloride (PVC) foam is widely used in various industries due to its lightweight structure, energy-absorbing capacity, and excellent mechanical properties. Understanding its behavior under different loading conditions is essential for optimizing its performance in applications such as impact protection [8], cushioning systems, and structural components [12].

As new technologies make it possible to produce increasingly complex cellular structures at lower costs [5], the use of functionally graded materials whose mechanical and physical properties vary spatially is gaining traction, depending on the specific application requirements [3, 9]. For foamed materials, one way to achieve such structures is to create a graded density distribution. However, for proper design and optimization of these materials, accurate characterization is necessary to enable reliable finite element simulations.

In this study, compression tests were conducted on PVC foam across a range of strain rates, from quasi-static to dynamic, and considering different nominal densities. This approach allowed for the evaluation of both strain rate effects and density-dependent behavior [7].

The experimental results were then used to calibrate the Ogden hyperelastic model [10], the Prony series for viscoelasticity, and the Mullins effect to account for foam damage and stress softening.

The goal of this work is to develop a user-defined constitutive model (VUMAT) capable of implementing all three models, thus accurately describing the behavior of PVC foam. Finally, an impact test simulation will be carried out on an absorber with a variable density distribution to verify the effectiveness of the VUMAT and assess the ability of graded-density structures to enhance energy absorption efficiency compared to an absorber with the same average density.

C. Sabbatini · G. Zandri · M. Sasso
Department of Mechanical Engineering, Università Politecnica delle Marche, Ancona, AN, 29208
Email: c.sabbatini@pm.univpm.it; g.zandri@staff.univpm.it; m.sasso@staff.univpm.it

Emily Retzlaff et al. (eds.), *Mechanics of Additive & Advanced Manufacturing, Inverse Methods and Machine Learning, Vol. 5*,
Conference Proceedings of the Society for Experimental Mechanics Series, https://doi.org/10.13052/9788743808312-6

Material and Experimental Tests

In this work, parallelepiped samples of closed cells PVC foam were tested to characterize the constitutive behavior of the material. We investigate the material response of commercial PVC foams with different densities, namely 130, 200 and 250 kg/m^3, provided by the company Diab and here indicated with their commercial name: Divinycell HP130, HP200 and HP250, respectively. These densities are selected to have foams with a high mechanical response and suitable for high-end applications, as the mechanical properties increase with foam density.

The tests were conducted in a wide range of nominal strain rate, i.e. 10^{-3}, 10^{-1}, 10^{1} and 10^{3} s^{-1}. All PVC foam samples have a nominal 12 mm $\times$ 12 mm square cross section. The length of the samples was 15 mm for the tests at 10^{-3} and 10^{-1} s^{-1}, while it was 10 mm for the ones tested at 10^{1} and 10^{3} s^{-1}; samples with different lengths were adopted to match the strain rate over the prescribed range according to our testing facilities.

All samples were tested in compression, with the load acting parallel to the growth (out-of-plane) direction. Three repetitions were carried out for each test condition, obtaining a strong repeatability of results; hence, only one curve for each test condition will be shown hereinafter. In addition, as expected for this class of material, a negligible lateral expansion was observed during compression tests.

We perform the compression tests at low and medium strain rate, from 10^{-3} to 10^{1} s^{-1} on a pneumatic testing machine, model Siplan® equipped with a 3 kN load cell. The machine piston can reach a speed of 100 mm/s. The tested samples were obtained from PVC planks of three different densities, i.e. 130, 200 and 250 kg/m^3, corresponding to 0.09, 0.14, and 0.18 relative density, respectively. In the low strain rate regime tests, i.e. 10^{-3} and 10^{-1} s^{-1}, the piston was gently moved downwards, approaching the upper sample surface, and the test started when the preload reached the value of 2 N. In the tests at medium strain rate (i.e. 10^{1} s^{-1}), the piston was moved to the uppermost position and accelerated from 0 to 100 mm/s before going into contact with the sample.

The dynamic tests were performed by means of the Split Hopkinson Pressure Bar (SHPB), whose calibration and adaptation to test soft materials are extensively described in [7, 8]. The SHPB apparatus is made up of three aligned bars named pre-stressed, input and output bars, which are 3.0, 7.5 and 4.0 m long, respectively. All bars have a diameter of 18 mm. A compression wave is produced inducing a sudden release of the elastic energy stored in the pre-stressed bar, which is statically pre-loaded by means of an electro mechanical actuator. This input wave travels through the input bar at the sound speed of the bar material and reaches the sample that is placed between the input and the output bars. While the sample is quickly deformed, the wave is partially transmitted to the output bar and partially reflected into the input bar. The strain induced by the incident, reflected and transmitted waves, respectively, is measured by strain gauge rosettes placed on the input and output bars in full Wheatstone bridge configuration. The signals obtained are used to compute the load at the two edges of the sample that are in contact with the input and output bars. The pre-stressed and input bars are made of aluminum (AA7075 T6) whereas, polyethylene terephthalate (PET) has been used for the output bar with the aim of increasing the sensitivity in the load measurement.

The experimental results, reported in Fig. 1, highlight the characteristic nonlinear behavior of foams, marked by an initial linear elastic region, followed by a stress plateau, and concluding with a densification phase. Furthermore, the mechanical response of the foams is strongly influenced by both density and strain rate: as these parameters increase, the plateau stress rises, and the onset of densification occurs at lower strains.

Costitutive Material Modelling

In this work, a user-defined constitutive model (VUMAT) was implemented to describe the material behavior, accounting simultaneously for the effects of density and strain rate. The following sections will provide a detailed description of the hyperelastic, viscoelastic models, the Mullins effect, and the variable density representation.

Hyper-elasticity

The hyperelastic model formulated by Ogden well describe the non-linear behavior of PVC foam. This model is available in the most commonly used finite element analysis software and is suitable for modeling both the static and time-dependent response of polymer foams. The model is based on the strain energy function, which depends on principal stretches, defined as $\lambda = L_f/L_0 = 1 + \epsilon$.

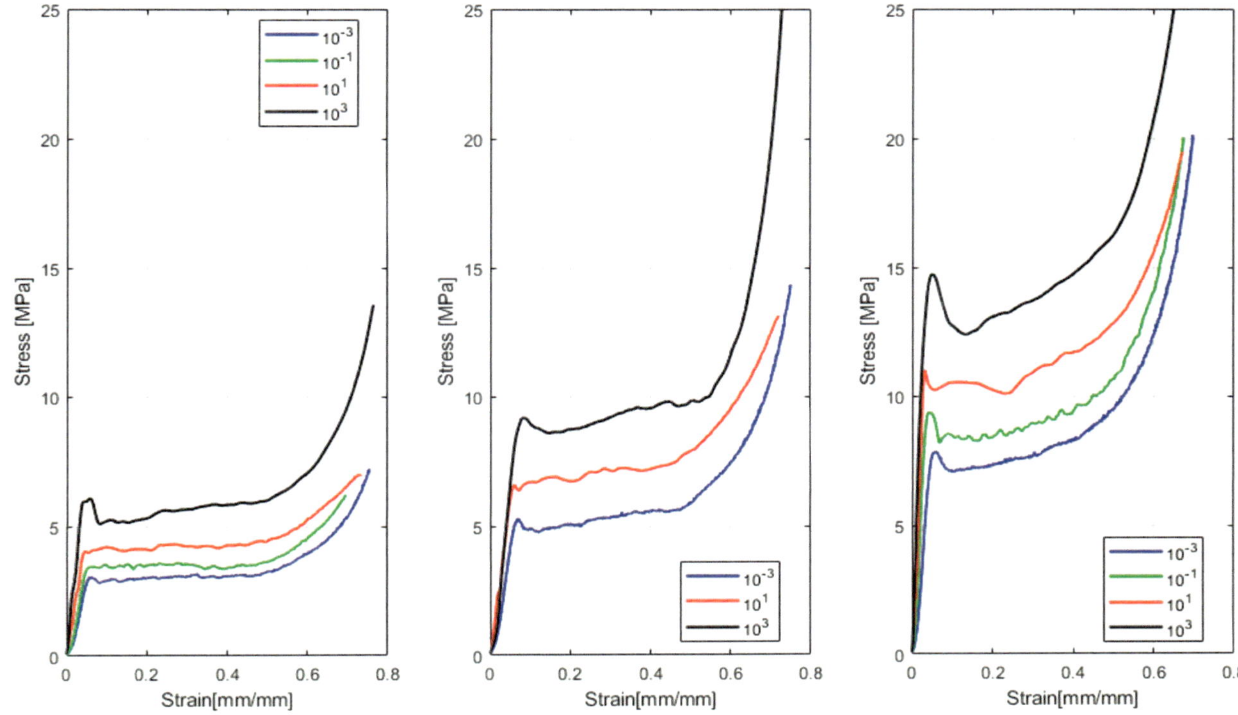

Fig. 1 Experimental compression test results, stress-strain curves

$$W(\lambda_1, \lambda_2, \lambda_3) = \sum_{i=1}^{N} \frac{2\mu_i}{\alpha_i^2} \left(\lambda_1^{\alpha_i} + \lambda_2^{\alpha_i} + \lambda_3^{\alpha_i} - 3 + \frac{1}{\beta_i}(J^{-\alpha_i\beta_1 - 1)} \right) \tag{1}$$

where N is the order of the model, J denotes the volume ratio (determinant of the deformation gradient F), μ_i, α_i, β_i are model parameters: μ_i has the unit of stress. In fact, it is directly correlated to the initial shear modulus G. Instead, α_i and β_i are both dimensionless, in particular α_i represents the hardening or softening exponent of the model and β_i is related to the effective Poisson's ratio ν.

$$G = \sum_{i=1}^{N} \mu_i \qquad \nu_i = \frac{\beta_i}{1 + 2\beta_i} \tag{2}$$

Starting from an hyperelastic strain energy potential W expressed according to the Ogden hyperfoam model, the principal stress of first Piola-Kirchhoff tensor P_k, can be obtained as:

$$\sigma = \frac{\partial W}{\partial \lambda_1} = \sum_{1=1}^{N} \frac{2\mu_i}{\alpha_i \lambda_1} (\lambda_1^{\alpha_i} - 1) \tag{3}$$

The Eq.(3) is used to fit the best parameters of the model using the quasi-static compression curve [6, 11].

Effect of density

To simulate the behavior of a functionally graded material,the parameters of the Ogden model were defined as a function of the generic density ρ,as shown in Eq. 4, based on the parameters calibrated from the mechanical behavior at a density of 130 kg/m^3.

$$
\begin{aligned}
\mu_{1,\rho} &= \mu_{1,130}\left(\frac{\rho}{\rho_{130}}\right)^{q_1}\\
\mu_{2,\rho} &= \mu_{2,130}\left(\frac{\rho}{\rho_{130}}\right)^{q_2}\\
\mu_{3,\rho} &= \mu_{3,130}\left(\frac{\rho}{\rho_{130}}\right)^{q_3}\\
\alpha_{i,\rho} &= \alpha_{i,130}
\end{aligned} \tag{4}
$$

The parameters q_i were obtained through optimization based on the experimental curves for densities of 200 and 250 kg/m^3, and the results are shown in Fig. 2. This density-dependent formulation, once implemented in the VUMAT, allows for the simulation of structures with a linearly varying density, rather than being limited to solids with layer-by-layer density variation [4].

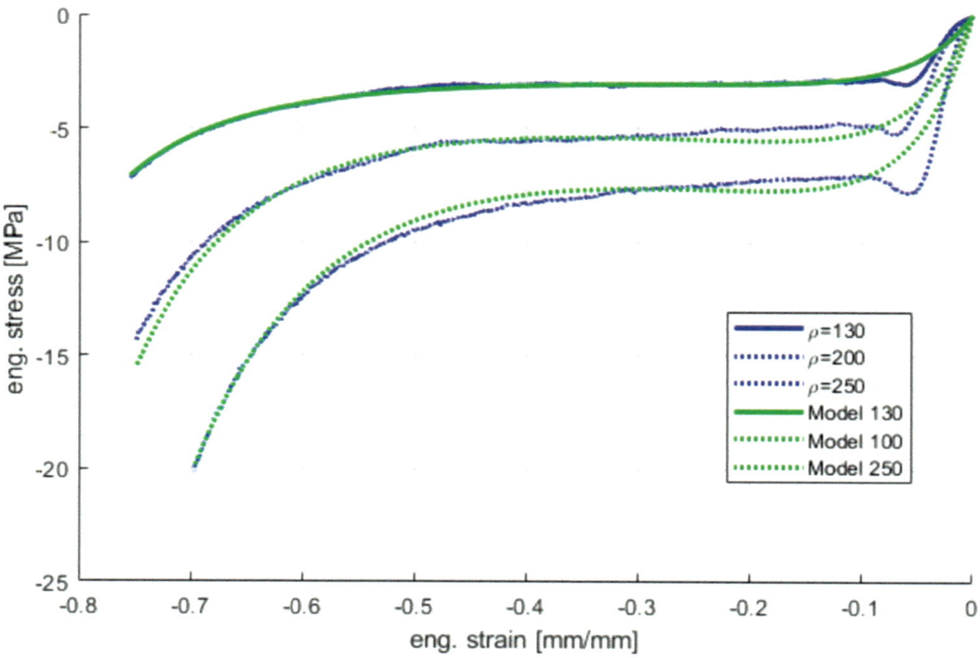

Fig. 2 Results of different density parameters fitting

Viscoelasticity and relaxation

The PVC foam shows a viscoelastic behavior that emerges in dynamic load conditions [13]. Consequently, the viscoelastic behavior must also be modeled in conjunction with the hyperelastic model. The Prony series (or generalized Maxwell) model was chosen. This model considers the material as a branch with a spring representing the long-term stiffness G_∞, in parallel with a series of N_G Maxwell branches, where a spring and a viscous damper are present. Each Maxwell branch is characterized by a relaxation time τ_i. The global relaxation modulus of such a system is given by:

$$
G(t) = G_0\left[g_\infty + \sum_{i=1}^{N_G}\left(g_i e^{-t/\tau_i}\right)\right] \tag{5}
$$

In Eq. (5), g_i are the relative moduli, so that $g_\infty + \sum g_i = 1$; G_0 represents the short term, or instantaneous, stiffness that is obtained as the sum of all branches' stiffness. The long term and short term stiffnesses are related as $G_\infty = g_\infty \cdot G_0$. The stress along time in the i-th layer of the Generalized Maxwell model is given by [2]:

$$
\left(\mathbf{S}_i^{2d}\right)_{n+1} = exp\left(-\frac{\Delta t}{\tau_i^G}\right)\left(\mathbf{S}_i^{2d}\right)_n + \alpha_i^G exp\left(-\frac{\Delta t}{2\tau_i^G}\right)\left[\frac{d\Phi}{d\mathbf{C}_{n+1}} - \frac{d\Phi}{d\mathbf{C}_n}\right] \tag{6}
$$

where $\mathbf{S}_i^{2d}$ is the second Piola-Kirchhoff stress tensor and $\mathbf{C}$ is the right Cauchy-Green deformation tensor. The true stress can be obtained from:

$$\sigma = \frac{2\mathbf{F}\mathbf{S}^{2d}\mathbf{F}^T}{J} \tag{7}$$

where $\mathbf{F}$ is the deformation gradient.

The total stress can be obtained from the sum of the hyperleastic stress with the N_G viscoelastic stresses.

In order to correctly model permanent energy dissipation effects and stress softening in PVC foam, Mullins effect is implemented, providing an extension to the elastomeric foam model [1]. Therefore, this damage model is used to include the damage present in elastomeric foams, modeling the energy absorption in foam components subjected to dynamic loading, with high strain rates compared to the characteristic relaxation time of the foam. In this model, energy dissipation effects are considered by introducing an augmented strain energy density function of the shape:

$$W(\lambda_i, \eta) = \eta W(\lambda_i) + \phi(\eta) \tag{8}$$

The function $W(\lambda_i, \eta)$ is a continuous function of the damage variable, η, and is related to the damage function $\phi(\eta)$. The damage variable, η, varies continuously during the course of deformation and always satisfies $0 < \eta < 1$, with $\eta = 1$ at the points of the primary curve (described by the Hyperfoam model). Taking into account the Mullins effect, the stresses are calculated by:

$$\sigma(\lambda_i, \eta) = \eta\sigma(\lambda_i) \tag{9}$$

where $\sigma(\lambda_i)$ is the stress corresponding to the primary behavior of the foam at the current strain level λ_i. Then, the stress is obtained by simply scaling the stress of the primary behavior of the foam by the damage variable η. Equation 9 is used when the material is at an energy potential W that is lower than the maximum energy potential W_m experienced by the material itself at the end of the loading phase. The damage variable is generally assumed to be represented by the so called "error function":

$$\eta = 1 - \frac{1}{r} erf\left(\frac{W_m - W}{m + \beta W_m}\right) \tag{10}$$

where r,m and β are material parameters that govern the shape of the unloading curve. Note that $r > 1$, $m \geq 0$, $\beta > 0$ [1].

Model validation

Before proceeding with the simulation of a puncture test, the proposed model was validated by reproducing the compression tests performed experimentally at different strain rates and densities. The specimen was modeled as a 2D body, constrained at the lower edge, applying the axial symmetry of the problem. Compression at various strain rates was applied by varying the velocity of the rigid body loading the PVC specimen. The simulation results for the density of 130 at strain rates of 10^{-3}, 10^1, and 10^3 are shown in Fig. 3a.

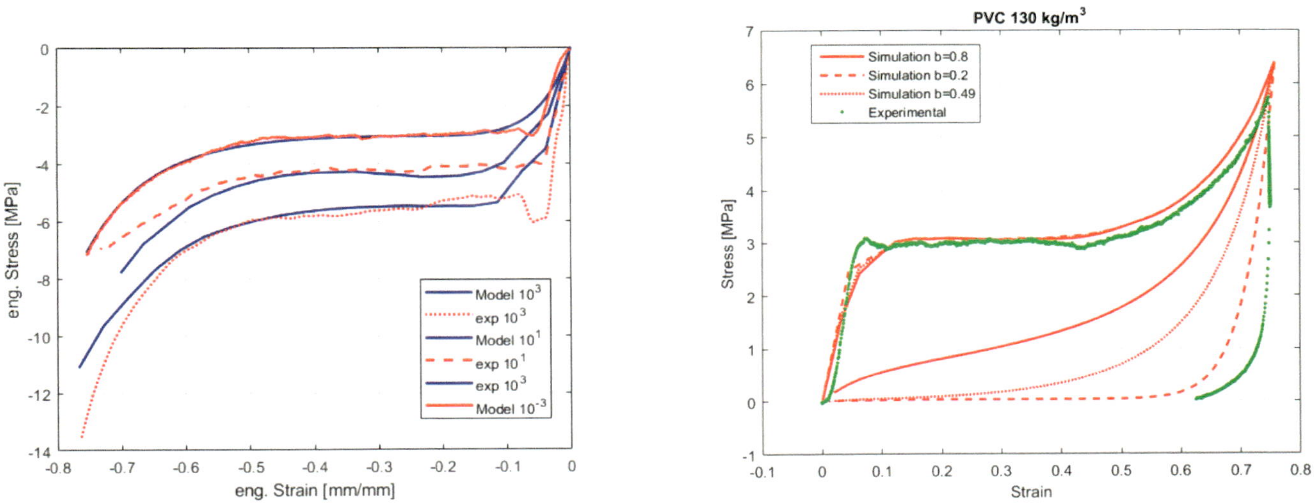

Fig. 3 (a)Hyperelastic and viscoelastic results,(b) Mullins effect result

The agreement between the experimental and numerical curves at the lowest strain rate validates the choice of the hyperelastic model parameters, while the good overlap of the curves at 10^1 and 10^3 demonstrates the ability of the Prony series model to capture the time-dependent behavior of the PVC foam. Fig. 3b shows the model behavior and the dependence of the Mullins effect on parameter β. Table 1 reports all the parameters used in the models.

Table 1 3th order Ogden hyperfoam parameters

μ_1	α_1	μ_2	α_2	μ_3	α_3	$\beta_{1\cdots4}$
1.463029	0.211745	-3.72722	0.859074	34.58817	21.63363	0

Table 2 Prony series with 10 terms parameters

τ_{min}	τ_{max}	g_1	g_2	g_3	g_4	g_5	g_6	g_7	g_8	g_9	g_{10}	g_∞
1E-5.783	1E3.367	0.0002	0.68	1.79E-06	1.76E-06	0.079	2.22E-06	0.0443	0.0083	0.0008	9.20E-07	0.188

Table 3 Mullins damage parameters

r	m	β
1.01	0.0001	0.2

Table 4 Density parameters

q_1	q_2	q_3
2.999	2.409	1.519

Puncture Test

A puncture test simulation was chosen to investigate and quantify the benefits of using a structure with variable density, focusing on evaluating the peak acceleration measured on the impactor during the test. To generate a large set of possible density distributions, a law was defined to distribute the density in an elliptical shape.

$$\Omega = \left| \left(\frac{X - x_c}{\frac{a}{n}} \right)^2 + \left(\frac{Y - y_c}{\frac{b}{n}} \right)^2 - 1 \right| \tag{11}$$

$$\rho_{min} + (\rho_{max} - \rho_{min}) \exp -\lambda\Omega \tag{12}$$

The first equation represent the location of the band with lower density, where x_c and y_c are the coordinates of the center of elliptical band, n is a factor that changes ellipse's axes dimensions and λ defines the band width. The Eq. 12 describe the density variation law. In order to compare the results obtained for various density distributions, it is necessary to keep the average density of the absorber unchanged and constant in every case. To achieve this, the parameter λ appearing in the distribution law was adjusted so that all density distributions had an average value of 200 kg/m^3. The impact tests were simulated by means of commercial Finite element software. In particular, the Abaqus/Explicit code was adopted because it is well suited for implementing user defined constitutive models. A 2D axisymmetric model of the PVC block impacted area and of impactor has been built. The PVC block is fixed on the bottom edge and meshed and the impactor is discretized as a rigid surface, with a 0.8 kg mass and an initial velocity equal to 10 m/s. The Fig. 4 show an example of our elliptical density distribution and three different moment of simulation.

As the final result of the simulation, the plot of the acceleration curves, Fig. 5, measured on the impactor is shown for the various density distribution cases, always compared with the uniform density case equal to the imposed equivalent density.

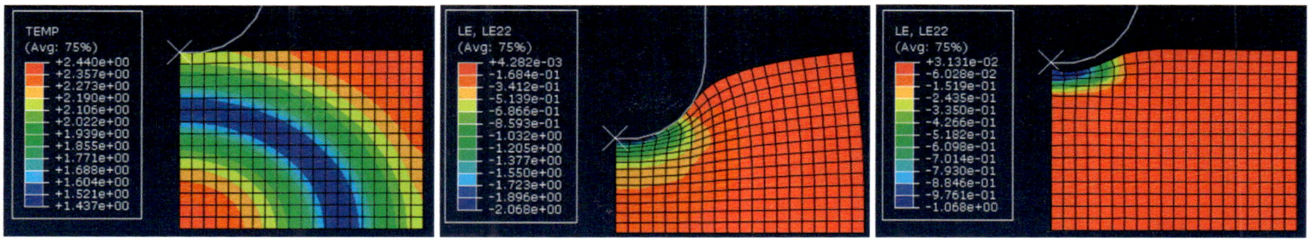

Fig. 4 Puncture test simulation (a)time = 0 with elliptical density distribution, (b) instant of maximum deformation, (c) residual deformation

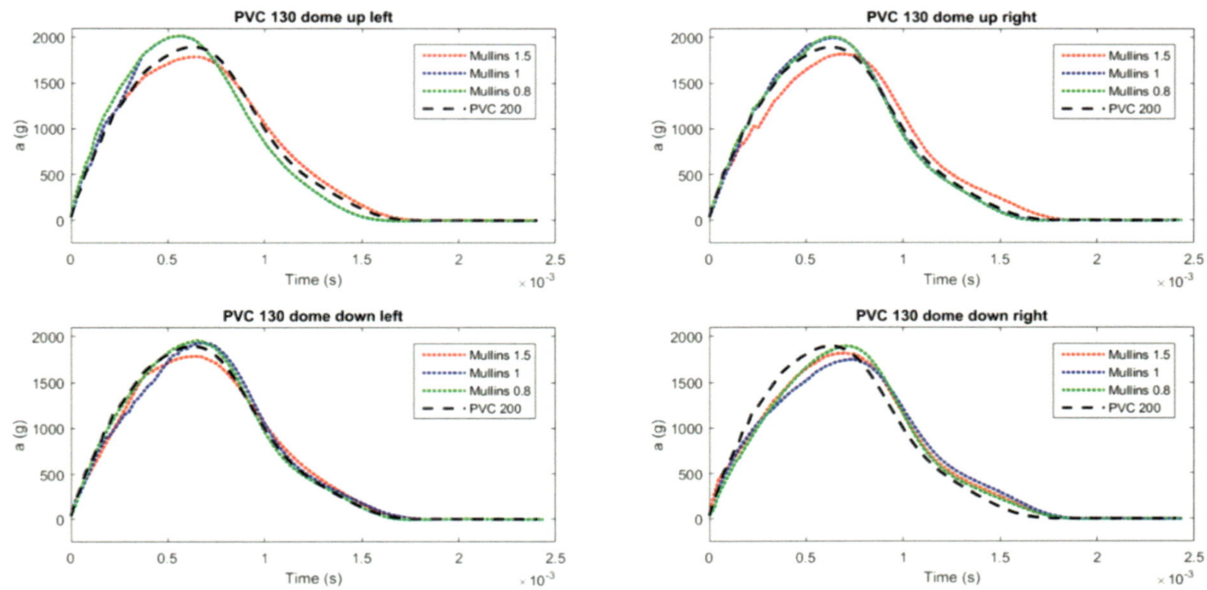

Fig. 5 Acceleration curves

Conclusions

In this work, compression tests on PVC foams with different densities, namely 130,200 and 250 kg/m^3, have been carried out at different strain rates, nominally from 10^{-3} to 10^3 s^{-1}. The tests were conducted by means of a servo pneumatic machine, exception made for the high strain rate tests performed by using a Split Hopkinson Pressure Bar, used to infer the stress-strain curves of the material.

Moreover, the stress-strain curves are used to calibrate a visco-elasto-plastic model, the minimization of an error function between the experimental and the analytical curves provides a reasonable estimation of parameters.

Once validated, the model is exploited to simulate the impact response of the foams under study. The simulation results in terms of acceleration curves show that the use of graded materials allows for improved energy absorption efficiency while keeping the average density of the absorber constant. Finally, the use of our defined model makes it possible to simultaneously implement both viscoelastic behavior and the Mullins effect, which is not always available in commercial Finite Element software.

References

1. 2022. *Help Abaqus*.
2. 2025 R1. *Help Ansys 2025*.
3. M.Alves D.Karagiozova. Propagation of compaction waves in cellular materials with continuosly varying density. *International Journal of Solids and Structures*, 2015.

4. A.H.Clausen O.s.Hopperstad D.T.Morton, A.Reyes. Mechanical response of low density expanded polypropylene foams in compression and tension at different loading rates and temperatures. *Materials Today Communications*, 2020.
5. S.Cardea E.Reverchon. Production of controlled polymeric foams by supercritical co2. *Supercritical Fluids*, 2007.
6. S. B. Attila Kossa. Novel strategy for the hyperelastic parameter fitting procedure of polymer foam material. *Polymer Testing*, 2016.
7. E.Mancini A.Lattanzi J.Tirillò C.Sergi M.Sasso, F.Sarasini. Wxperimental characterization and numerical modelling of the impat behavior of pvc foams. *Experimental Mechanics*, 2023.
8. A.Kmetty M.Tomin. Polymer foams as advanced energy absorbing materials for sports applications. *Journal of Applied Polymer Science*, 2021.
9. S.Kumar M.Utzeri, H.cebeci. Autonomous sensing architected materials. *Advanced Functional Material*, 2024.
10. R.Ogden. Large deflection isotropi elasticity - on the correletion of theory and experiment for incompressible rubberlike solids.
11. D. J. Y. Y. L. W. Y. Q. Q. W. Shunping Yan. Novel strategies for parameter fittin procedure of the ogden hyperfoam model under shear condition. *European Journal of Mechanics /A Solids*, 2021.
12. B.Depreitere J Ivens J.V.Sloten Y.Mosleh, M. Cajka. Smart material and design solutions for protective headgears in linear and oblique impacts. *Smart Materials and Structures*, 2023.
13. X.Zhang X.An Y.Xiong Y.Sun Y.Xiao, J.Yin. Mechanical performance and cushioning energy absorption characteristics of rigid polyurethane foam at low and high strain rates. *Polymer testing*, 2022.

Chapter 7
Design, Fabrication and Characterization of Layered Jamming Bistable Composite Structures for Assistive Robotics

Hugh A. Bruck, Supriya Shastry, and Oliver J. Myers

Abstract There is growing interest in developing assistive robotic structures, such as exoskeletons, for a variety of potential applications, such as rehabilitation robotics. Advanced structural and material concepts, such as layered jamming and bistable composites, are providing new opportunities to engineer assistive robotic structures that can employ mechanics principles that allow for new approaches to controlling these structures to achieve better outcomes than conventional robotic platforms employing traditional machine components (e.g., servo motors, linear actuators, etc.). New manufacturing and design processes employing 3d printing, digital twins, and Artificial Intelligence are also providing new opportunities to rapidly realize new systems that employ advanced structures and materials. We have recently investigated the fabrication, design, and characterization of a model assistive robotic structures employing advanced structural and material concepts to achieve novel control of the robot's mechanical behavior relative to the plant's behavior.

Keywords Bistable composites · Layered jamming · Hysteresis · Morphing · Vacuum pressure

Introduction

There is increasing interest in creating lightweight morphing structures that can be deployed in a variety of applications, including soft robotics, vibration control, medical devices, material handling, and aerospace. One approach we have recently pursued for realizing morphing structures, primarily for robotic platforms, is layered jamming [1–4]. This technique involves stacking multiple material layers and using differential pressure to modulate the friction between them, thereby enabling real-time control over the mechanical properties of a structure. There have been a variety of techniques developed for controlling properties of materials in situ, including electro-programming, thermal actuation, and magnetic fields. The ability to vary properties in situ has become crucial in the field of soft robotics, where both flexibility and stiffness are required in applications such as grippers, exoskeletons, and aerospace [5, 6]. However, layered jamming offers several advantages over alternative approaches, including variable stiffness through rapid transitions between flexible and rigid states, minimal volumetric change, simple fabrication, and a high strength-to-weight ratio. These properties make it particularly well-suited for applications requiring tunable stiffness.

In parallel, recent advancements in bistable structures, such as those composed of asymmetric layups of laaminated carbon fiber composites, have enabled the development of structures capable of maintaining two distinct equilibrium states for applications, such as robotics, including bistable structures with a tunable response and Kirigami bistable composites [7, 8]. Bistable structures have been widely studied for their ability to achieve rapid energy release and force amplification. For carbon fiber composites, the bistability arises from an orthogonal and asymmetric curing configuration of unidirectional carbon fiber layers, which induces an internal bending moment due to the residual stress distribution that can last for millions of cycles [9]. However, traditional bistable composites typically operate between two fixed states, limiting their adaptability. Recent work has shown that intermediate states with tunable energy barriers can significantly expand their

Hugh A. Bruck
Department of Mechanical Engineering, University of Maryland, College Park, MD
e-mail: bruck@umd.edu

Oliver J. Myers
Department of Mechanical Engineering, Clemson University, Clemson, SC
e-mail: omyers@clemson.edu

Emily Retzlaff et al. (eds.), *Mechanics of Additive & Advanced Manufacturing, Inverse Methods and Machine Learning, Vol. 5*,
Conference Proceedings of the Society for Experimental Mechanics Series, https://doi.org/10.13052/9788743808312-7

functionality, enabling more precise control over deformation and response. Additionally, bistable structures are inherently energy efficient, as they rely on stored elastic energy rather than continuous actuation, making them promising candidates for applications requiring low-power operation. While actuation methods such as magnetic fields, thermal activation, and electroactive materials have been explored, vacuum-based control provides a highly efficient and reversible approach for modulating mechanical properties in real time. Despite these advantages, relatively few studies have explored how integrating bistability with passive material systems—such as layered jamming—could enable reconfigurable structures with tunable mechanical properties for applications, such as exoskeletons for assistive robotics.

To address this gap, we investigate the integration of layered jamming with bistable laminated composites and examine how the mechanical interaction between the two layers is influenced by vacuum pressure when they are jammed. Two bistable composite plates, one with a 3D printed mechanism to induce a biasing force to allow recovery between the two stable states, were stacked on top of each other in the stable state with maximum curvature and with the axes of curvature collinear and the curved surfaces facing in the same direction. The specimens were placed in a bag and tested in three-point bending with the vacuum pressure being varied up until a full vacuum. The resulting data was compared with a model we previously developed for layered jamming composites.

Experimental Method

Layered jamming structure with bistable composites.

For this investigation, we fabricated structures using two bistable composite plates made from unidirectional carbon fiber lamina. The plates were 150 mm × 150 mm in-plane, and had a $0_2/90_2$ and the other a 0/90 ply layup for thicknesses of 0.8 mm and 0.4 mm respectively. A mechanism was designed to be 3-D printed and attached to the bottom of the $0_2/90_2$ plate to constrain it from deforming, and enabling it to reverse from the deformed to the initiate stable state through the biasing moment. The two bistable composite plates can be seen in *Figure 1* from the bottom surface of the plates, with the thicker plate inverted to display the 3D printed biasing mechanism. The curvature can be seen in the side view in Figure 1. It is

Top View

Side View

Fig. 1 Two bistable composite plates that were used for layered jamming experiments (biased plate with biasing mechanism is on the right).

clear that the curvature for the 0/90 plate results in a height that is twice that of the $0_2/90_2$ plate. To fabricate the jammed structures, we placed the plates in the stable state with maximum curvature on top of each other with the axis of curvature collinear and the curvature facing in the same direction. The plates were then placed inside a vacuum bag for testing.

Three-point bend mechanical testing

To characterize the effects of vacuum pressure and cyclic loading, we performed three point bend tests with just two opposing corners of the plate specimen pinned and the central load applied to the center of the surface of the plate using a Bose Electroforce test frame. The degree of deformation exhibited by a bistable laminated composite is very sensitive to boundary conditions, therefore we built a three point-bending test rig that would enable us to control the distribution of the clamping force in order to characterize the mechanical behavior of the layered jamming structure using conditions that range from clamped to pinned (*Figure 2*). A vacuum is drawn inside the bag by using a electric vacuum pump at a rate of 1.6 L/sec with the vacuum pressure measured using a Hardware Factory Store 8542039686 vacuum gauge. A valve was used to control the vacuum pressure from -3 kPa to a full vacuum. shown in Figure 2. The displacement and load data were obtained at a sampling rate of 1000 Hz. Experiments were conducted from vertical displacements of 0 mm at the unloaded state to -21 mm of displacement over 10 cycles at 1 Hz.

Fig. 2 Three-point bending test with layer jamming bistable composite specimen.

Modeling Mechanical Behavior in Three-point Bending

Previously, we developed the following model based on Euler-Bernoulli equations to predict the mechanical behavior of a layered jamming structure. First, we relate the change in strains, ε_i, between layers to the displacement discontinuity at the interface due to slip, du_i, along the axial location, x.

$$\varepsilon_{o,i} + kt_i - \varepsilon_{o,i+1} = \frac{du_i(x)}{x}$$

We can then determine the strain at the bottom of the first layer from the slip and the curvature of the structure, k, and thickness of each layer t_i, as follows:

$$\varepsilon_{o,1}h = -\sum_{i=1}^{N}\left[\frac{k(x)t_i^2}{2}\right] - \sum_{i=2}^{N}\sum_{j=2}^{i} t_i\left[kt_{j-1} - \frac{du_{j-1}(x)}{x}\right]$$

To achieve equilibrium, we relate the corresponding internal stress distribution to the applied bending moment, M, and the internal balance of force from the transverse location of each interface, h_i, as follows:

$$M(x) = Eb\sum_{i=1}^{N} \left[-\frac{k(x)}{3}\left({h_{i+1}}^3 - {h_i}^3\right) + \frac{(k(x)h_i + \varepsilon_{o,i})}{2}\left({h_{i+1}}^2 - {h_i}^2\right)\right]$$

$$0 = \sum_{i=1}^{N} \left[-\frac{k(x)}{2}\left({h_{i+1}}^2 - {h_i}^2\right) + (k(x)h_i + \varepsilon_{o,i})\left(h_{i+1} - h_i\right)\right]$$

From the Euler-Bernoulli model, the maximum shear stress occurs in the center of the cross section of the beam and is given by:

$$\tau_{max} = 1.5\frac{\mathrm{V}}{\mathrm{A}}$$

where V is the shear force and A is the cross-sectional area. Interlayer shear stress, τ_{inter} is given by:

$$\tau_{\text{inter },i} = \frac{3V}{2A}\left[1 - \left(\frac{2y_i}{h} - 1\right)^2\right]$$

Where h is the total thickness of the layer jamming specimen. The maximum interlayer shear stress that can be sustained by jamming layers with surface friction coefficient, under a vacuum pressure is given by:

$$\tau_{\text{inter }\_max} = \mu\Delta P$$

Therefore, the maximum load, V_{max}, before slip occurs at an interface located at y_i:

$$V_{\text{max}} = \frac{2A\mu\Delta P}{3\left[1 - \left(\frac{2y_i}{h} - 1\right)^2\right]}$$

For our experiments, one of the specimens was biased by a mechanism to induces a constraint on the lower surface that prevents it from stretching, and imposes a bending moment opposing the loading so that the lower surface of the structure has zero strain. The resulting biased bistable composite plate has an impact on the resulting stiffness reduction for the layered jamming bistable composite structure when slip occurs at the interface between the bistable composite plates. We again can look at this from a 1-D perspective using the previous Euler-Bernoulli beam theory, where for the two layer jammed bistable composite structure with plate thickness h_1 and h_2, respectively, the bending stiffness, $(EI)_{c,jam}$, is related to the bending stiffnes of each layer, $(EI)_1$ and $(EI)_1$, as follows:

$$(EI)_{c,jam} = (EI)_1 + 4E{h_1}^3/b + (EI)_2 + E(h_1 + 0.5h_2)^2\, h_2 b$$

When there is slip at the interface, their stiffness becomes:

$$(EI)_{c,jam} = (EI)_1 + 4E{h_1}^3/b + (EI)_2$$

Since the constraint is applied on the first plate to create the biased response. Thus, the resulting stiffness reduction ratio, $(EI)_{c,ratio}$, can be determined as follows:

$$(EI)_{c,ratio} = [(EI)_1 + 0.25E{h_1}^3/b + (EI)_2]/[(EI)_1 + E{h_1}^3/(4b) + (EI)_2 + E(h_1 + 0.5h_2)^2\, h_2 b]$$

For our specimens, $h_1 = 2\, h_2$, therefore, the stiffness reduction ratio should be 3.3.

Experimental Results

Three-point bending of layered jamming bistable composites

For the initial set of experiments, we used three-point bending to characterize the behavior of the two bistable composite plates stacked on top of each other in the stable state with maximum curvature with the directions of curvature collinear. The inherent load-displacement behavior for the biased bistable composite plate can be seen in *Figure 3* (seen in wide black in the figure, we only tested the biased plate, since it maintains contact during the entire compressive displacement range that we tested through the bistable response region. The response of the two jammed bistable composite plates can also be seen in Figure 3 with vacuum pressures as low as -3 kPa all the way (designated in wide red) to a full vacuum. It can be seen that at -3 kPa, the response represents the combination of the two bistable composite plates. As the vacuum pressure increases, the hysteresis loop expands as the jammed bistable composite plates stiffen by increasing the energy level associated with the instability to make it more difficult to initiate the plate buckling response.

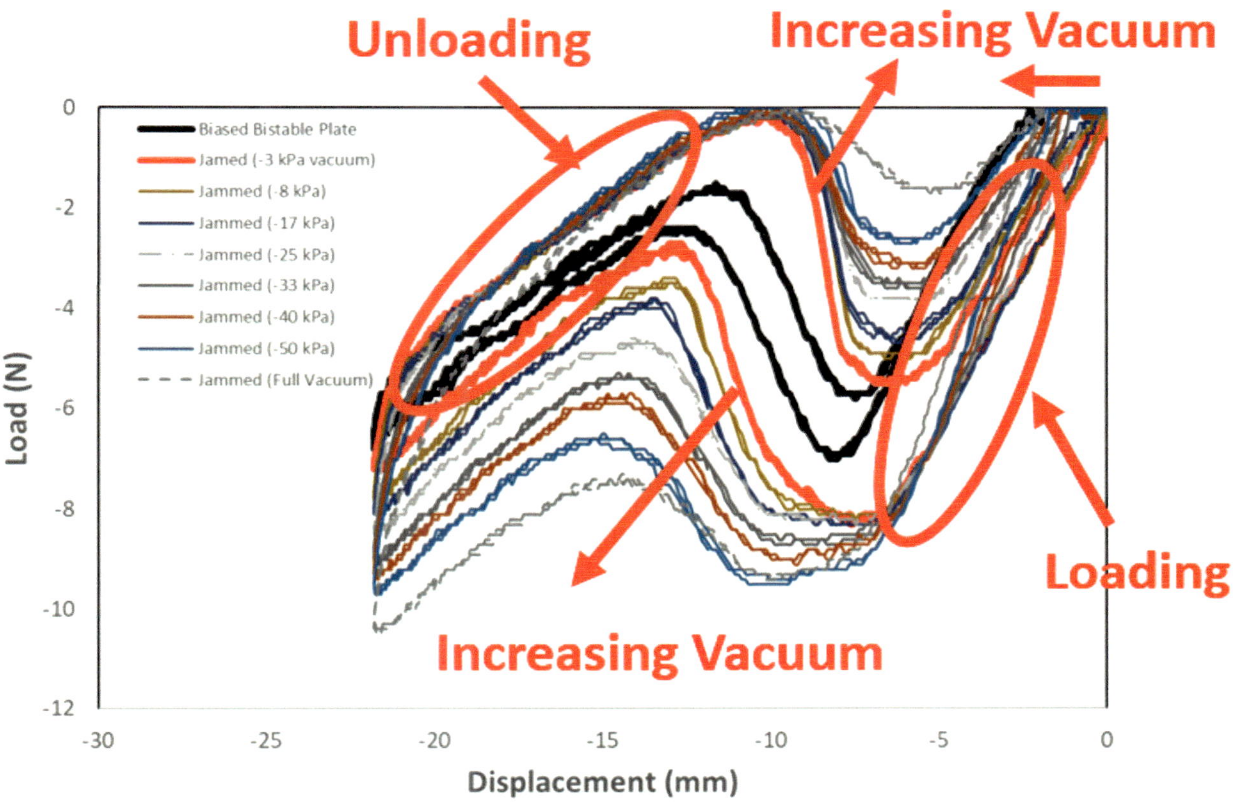

Fig. 3 Experimental results obtained in three-point bending for two jammed layered bistable composite plates starting at -3 kPa of vacuum pressure (wide red) all the way to a full vacuum, as compared to the biased bistable composite plate.

The increase in hysteresis with vacuum pressure can be attributed to the maximum shear force that was expected at the interface. It can be seen that the minimum load after the buckling instability is initiated upon loading goes from near the response of the biased bistable composite plate at -2.9 N when there is -3 kPa of vacuum pressure all the way to -7.4 N at full vacuum. From the model, the expected shear load resistance at full vacuum pressure would be increasing from 0 N up to 4.5 N for a coefficient of friction of 0.24 at the interface between the bistable composite plates. Thus, it appears the vacuum pressure is controlling that dip in load based on the vacuum pressure. Thus, it is possible to control the bistable response to adjust to the desired needs of the patients. At higher pressures, there is a much lower negative stiffness, which increases the interaction distance with patients.

It was also noted that as the vacuum pressure increased, the load approached 0 before the buckling instability initiated when the jammed plates were unloaded. Initially, the adhesion of the two plates induced by layer jamming is sufficient to treat the structures as one continuous structure with stiffness associated with the combined thicknesses. This "tightening up" of the structure can also be seen as the initial displacement for three-point bend loading decreases with increasing vacuum pressure, which decreases to -2.19 mm. That stiffened response was maintained until a level of -6 N was reached. At that point, the response separates with increasing take-off stiffness with increasing vacuum pressure. The same tightening effect can also be seen as the plates are unloaded, until they approach 0 N at approximately -12 mm, at which point the take-off response upon buckling becomes more compliant with increasing vacuum pressure until the specimen is fully unloaded. Clearly, this indicates that the specimen is starting to approach a state where there is residual energy left to initiate reverse buckling and allow the plates to deform. In fact, the plates tended to stay deformed after 10 cycles at a displacement of approximately -12 mm as the vacuum pressure increased, as seen in Figure 4. The unloading and loading bath had an initial slope similar to the slope upon initial loading during the first cycle. At -4.5 N of loading, the specimen exhibits a reduction in stiffness of 2.6X, which is close to what was expected based on the modeling prediction without the instability, which is also shown in *Figure 4.* This slope is also slightly greater than the slope observed after the instability is initiated upon loading and unloading. For applications such as exoskeletons for assistive robotics, this would equate to a time-dependent response that would initiate under the right cyclic loading condition to activate either a permanent decoupling of the structure from the patient, or a permanent grasping force.

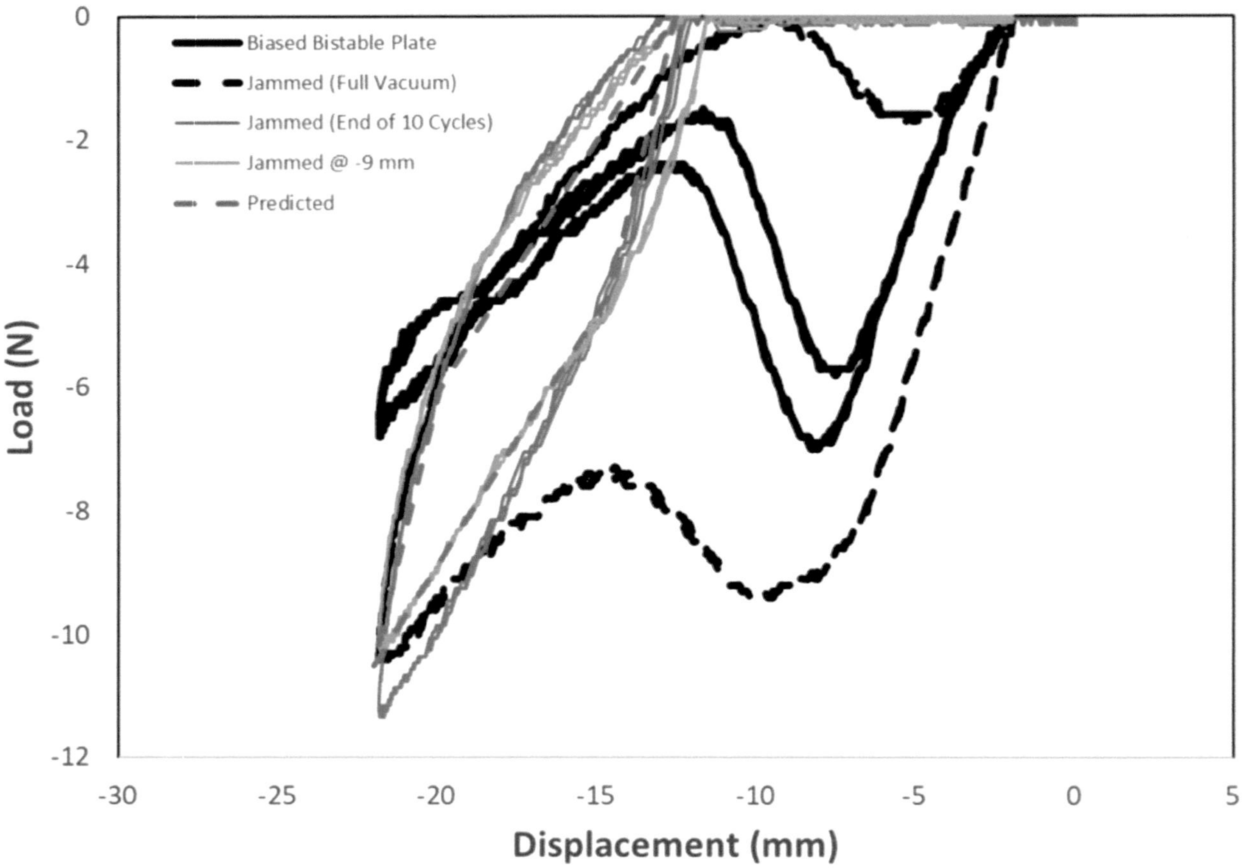

Fig. 4 Experimental results obtained in three-point bending for two layered bistable composite plates jammed at full vacuum pressure initially and after 10 cycles of loading. The resulting response of the specimen with vacuum pressure applied at -12 mm to jam it is nearly identical, as is the predicted response from the modeling.

Morphing behavior of layered jamming bistable laminated composites

One of the interesting aspects of the layered jamming bistable laminated composites was the ability to retain plastic deformation at elevated vacuum pressures to "lock in" a deformed state at -12 mm of displacement when activated by cycling loading, as seen in *Figure 5.* Of course, upon reducing the vacuum pressure, the specimen would initiate recovery to the original undeformed state at a vacuum pressure of approximately -25 kPa. This also correlated to when the load upon unloading reached 0 with increasing vacuum pressure to this level, as seen previously in Figure 3. This morphing behavior can be seen below in Figure 5. It also provides another mechanism for controlling the interaction of a structure with the patient, allowing the deformed response to be initiated upon cycling loading, and then deactivated upon reducing the vacuum pressure. This ability to reverse plastic deformation is very similar to a shape memory material, where the mechanism in this case is vacuum pressure.

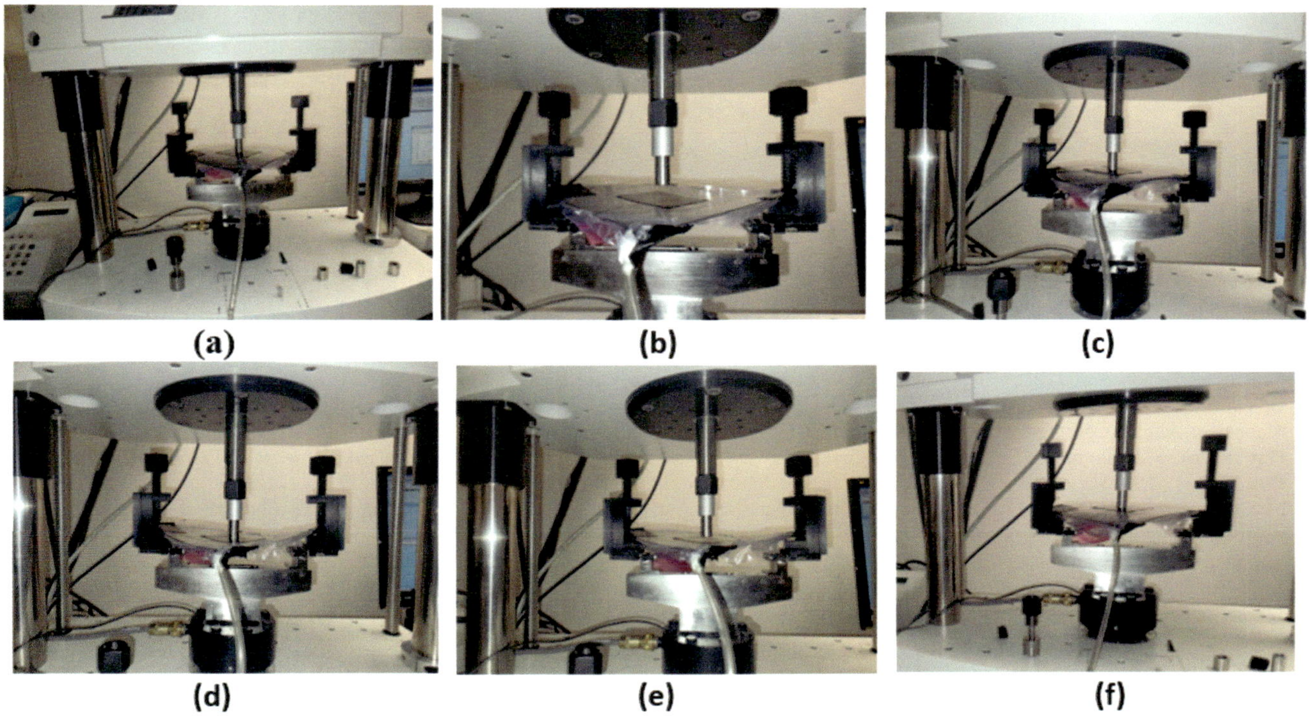

Fig. 5 Morphing behavior of two layered bistable composite structure jammed at full vacuum pressure: (a) before cycling loading, (a) after cycling at 1 Hz for 10 cycles., (c) after reducing vacuum to below -25 kPa, (d) deforming the specimen to -12 mm and drawing a full vacuum, (e) after unloading, (f) after reducing the vacuum to below -25 kPa.

Conclusions

We have recently characterized layered jamming structures consisting of layered bistable laminated composites, in order to understand how layered jamming can be used to create novel lightweight morphing structures for various applications, such as assistive robotics. The bistable laminated composite is capable of transitioning between two stable shapes and can be combined together or with passive elements through layered jamming, the bistable behavior can be controlled using vacuum pressure, resulting in morphing behavior that is similar to a shape memory material. Specimens were fabricate from two composite bistable plates made from carbon fiber/epoxy lamina, with two different layups to induce different levels of curvature. A stiff 3D printed structure was attached to one side of the plate with the lower curvature in order to prevent the surface from deforming and therefore inducing a reverse bending moment that could reverse the structure from the second stable state back to the original stable state upon unloading. It was observed that as the vacuum pressure increased, the hysteresis increased, as stiffness after the instability initiated due to slip at the interface. A similar trend was observed upon unloading. However, as the pressure increased to full vacuum, the load would reach 0 N upon unloading, and the specimen would stay in a permanently deformed state at the end of 10 cycles. The specimen would then exhibit similar cycling behavior without the instability as it would if the specimen had the vacuum drawn after it had been deformed to -12 mm without a vacuum. The change in the minimum load observed after the instability is initiated upon loading and unloading correlated to the increase in loading that would be required to overcome the frictional force, which is proportional to the vacuum pressure, at the interface between the plates. This vacuum-controlled stiffness allows for novel implementation for impedance control of assistive robotics, where itis possible to control the bistable response to adjust to the desired needs of a patient. The cyclic behavior in the permanently deformed state also correlated to model predictions without the instability. The permanently deformation could be recovered by reducing the vacuum pressure below -25 kPa. This enabled the structure to exhibit morphing behavior similar to a shape memory material, where it could be used to control the interactions with a patient for assistive robotic applications, such as exoskeletons, where it can activate either a permanent decoupling of the structure from the patient, or a permanent grasping force.

Acknowledgments The authors are grateful for the support from DEVCOM Army Research Laboratory (DEVCOM ARL) sponsors of this research under Cooperative Agreement W911NF2020222 with the University of Maryland entitled UMD-ARL Alliance for Additive Manufacturing Science. The fndings reported here should not be construed as an of?cial DEVCOM ARL position unless so indicated by other authorized documentation.

References

1. R. Acevedo, L. Santos, R. D. Pederson, N. Goyal, N.M. Bruck, S.K. Gupta, and H.A. Bruck, ""Characterization and Modeling of Layer Jamming for Designing Materials with Programmable Elastic-Plastic Behavior", Experimental Mechanics, DOI: 10.1007/s11340-020-00618-0 (2020).
2. H. A. Bruck, R. Acevedo, J. Rohwerder, L. Johnson, and S.K. Gupta, "Layered Jamming Multifunctional Actuators", Proceedings of the Society for Experimental Mechanics Annual Conference and Exposition, Greenville SC, 1-11 (2018).
3. H.A .Bruck, N.M. Bruck, R. Acevedo, and S.K. Gupta, "Fatigue of Layered Jamming Materials, Proceedings of the Society for Experimental Mechanics Annual Conference and Exposition, Pittsburgh, PA, 1-7 (2022)
4. H.A .Bruck, S. Millman, E. Beyene, M. Deshmukh, and O.J. Myers, "Layered Jamming Functional Polymer-Based Composite Structures, Proceedings of the Society for Experimental Mechanics Annual Conference and Exposition, Orlando, FL, 1-8 (2023)
5. M. Shen, A.B. Clark, and N. Rojas, "A scalable variable stiffness revolute joint based on layer jamming for robotic exoskeletons", In: Mohammad, A., Dong, X., Russo, M. (eds) Towards Autonomous Robotic Systems. TAROS 2020. Lecture Notes in Computer Science, 12228. Springer, Cham. https://doi.org/10.1007/978-3-030-63486-5_1 (2020)
6. A. M. El-Sayed, "A novel approach to enhancing smart stiffness of soft robotic gripper fingers for wider grasping capability", International Journal of Intelligent Robotics and Applications, https://doi.org/10.1007/s41315-024-00398-z, 1-21 (2024)
7. Y. Jiang, Y. Li, K. Liu, H. Zhang, X. Tong, D. Chen, and J. Paik, "Ultra-tunable bistable structures for universal robotic applications", Cell Reports Physical Science, 4(5) (2023)
8. A. Lele, V. Deshpande, O. Myers, and S. Li, "Snap-through and stiffness adaptation of a multi-stable Kirigami composite module", Composites Science and Technology, 182, 107750 (2019)
9. S.A. Chowdhury, S. Li, and O.J. Myers, "Fatigue analysis of bistable composite laminate", Smart materials, adaptive structures and intelligent systems 86274, V001T02A005 (2022)

Chapter 8
Assessing the Effects of Strain Rate, Print Orientation and Post Print Annealing in FDM PLA Specimens in an Undergraduate Materials Science Course

Matt Schaefer

Abstract This paper describes the development of a lab experiment for an undergraduate Materials Science course which demonstrates the influence of print orientation, strain rate and post-print annealing in FDM specimens of PLA polymer. The objective of experimentation in a materials science course is for students to have firsthand experience with common material property tests and understand how design properties are determined from those tests. But materials selection is a first step, not the end of story. A stretch goal is to understand some subtle factors beyond just designing to tensile, yield, and % elongation from a standard test. This experiment utilized tensile test specimens that were created via FDM using three different print orientations. This provided a clear demonstration of the anisotropic nature tensile properties in FDM. As expected, cross-layer mechanical properties are significantly reduced in specimens tested across print layers. In a second part of the experiment, influence of strain rate (testing at 0.5, 15 and 500 mm/min) was successfully demonstrated, with 20% higher tensile strength and lower elongation for the highest strain rate. Additionally, some samples were annealed after printing to improve mechanical properties. Results for this were mixed and mostly demonstrated the practical difficulties with trying to improve properties of PLA printed parts via heat treatment. For students, this lab was effective for the target objective and the stretch goal: they correctly analyzed tensile results and started to appreciate some of the finer points of material selection within mechanical design.

Keywords Fused Deposition Modeling · Tensile Test · PLA · Strain Rate · Print Orientation

Introduction

The idea that students learn best in their preferred learning style is not backed up by the research. Far more effective is to present concepts using a combination of teaching modes. Even more important is to suitably match the mode of delivery to specific course topics [1] [2]. Materials Science is well suited to experimentation for course topics involving concepts we can see and feel and test. These would include: How are polymers different than metals? What are mechanical properties and how do we test them? These questions are the focal points for an experiment involving tensile testing of FDM printed SLA polymer specimens. The course in Materials Science 1 is required third year course in the mechanical engineering program at Milwaukee School of Engineering (MSOE). A follow-on course, Materials & Manufacturing Processes is also required.

A good basic experiment will support a lecture topic with a physical demonstration of some principle of materials science in line with stated course learning objectives. And in this case, the "ability to perform experiments" is also a stated course outcome. A great experiment will go beyond this basic approach. Curriculum is a continuum, and experiments provide a good opportunity to review material learned in prerequisite courses and to preview material that students may study in future courses. Planning a lab-lesson can follow three basic questions; 1) What do we know already? 2) What are we learning today? 3) How does this lead into things you will learn in the future? As an example, mechanics of materials is prerequisite course for materials science. Students already know the concept of Young's modulus and that it describes elastic behavior up the yield. Or does it? When watching a tensile test in progress, there is time to point out that the "linear" portion may not really be so close to linear. When is this important? If those students take a future course in Fatigue & Fracture in

Matt Schaefer
Department of Mechanical Engineering, Milwaukee School of Engineering, 1025 N. Broadway, Milwaukee WI 53202 USA
e-mail: schaefma@msoe.edu

Emily Retzlaff et al. (eds.), *Mechanics of Additive & Advanced Manufacturing, Inverse Methods and Machine Learning, Vol. 5*,
Conference Proceedings of the Society for Experimental Mechanics Series, https://doi.org/10.13052/9788743808312-8

Mechanical design, they will learn that this “slight” deviation (which occurs below yielding) is the key factor in describing the accumulation of fatigue damage in metals. These points are part of the in-lab discussion.

The same past-present-future approach applies within the course. One course learning outcome for the materials science is: Identify typical properties… for broad categories of materials (metals, polymers, ceramics, and composites). A week-1 course assignment was to simply do MatWeb research and compare mechanicals for metals versus polymers versus ceramics [3]. In a week’s prior experiment, students did tensile testing on metals. Following up with tests run on polymer samples provides the physical demonstration of the differences: 1) polymers are much lower strength and lower modulus materials, 2) polymers can be strain-rate sensitive, 3) polymers are, in general, more non-linear from the start of the stress-strain response. These three points support the primary course objective, to answer what is different about polymers versus metals. The second half of the materials course sequence concentrates more on manufacturing processes. Consideration of fabrication method and post-processing (FDM printing, print orientation as an experiment variable, post-print annealing) are not really necessary for the objectives of the basic materials 1 course. But these concepts do support course objectives for the follow-on manufacturing course.

Background

The lab experiment, which is the subject of this paper, aims to demonstrate typical mechanical properties of polymers. This could be accomplished using injection molded or machined test specimens. However, basing the experiment on 3D printed specimens helps spur interest and curiosity in the students. Simple FDM printers using PLA polymer are familiar to all the students, and many have made parts via this method. Tensile testing is the most fundamental technique for obtaining important design properties of strength, ductility and elastic modulus. The method used here follows closely to the ASTM D638 Standard Test Method for Tensile Testing of Plastics [4]. To expand beyond the basics, three additional elements were added to the experiment, effect of print orientation, effect of strain rate, and possible improvement of properties by post-print annealing.

With FDM printing, it is a well understood phenomenon that the mechanical properties will depend on print direction. The nature of the print method will produce incomplete bonding between successive layers as well as residual flaws or voids in the layering. These factors result in lower strength and elongation in tensile properties. Much data is available in the literature. Some FDM filament suppliers will provide data regarding this influence. Overture technical data sheet for PLA [5] shows tensile strength as 47.1 MPa in X-Y directions (lateral) and 38.9 MPa in the Z direction (vertical). Modulus, however, is only reported in the lateral direction, as E = 2641 MPa. Another supplier for materials used in this study, Polymaker - PolyLite™ PLA [6], gives tensile strength at 52.3 MPa in X-Y directions versus 40.5 MPa in Z direction, and also E = 3426 MPa in X-Y direction versus E = 3064 MPa in Z direction. It is expected that the current experiment would show similar results with those two materials. However, the current experiment explores the concept of “directionality” in a slightly different manner. Printing a flat tensile specimen flat to the printing platen, but in a different orientation is what the suppliers would refer to as X or Y. In the current study, an option of printing the flat sample but with the edge towards the platen is considered. This variation could be important when applying test results to practical parts made via FDM.

Polymers are more sensitive to changes in strain rate compared to other classes of material. Generally, increasing strain rate will increase both tensile strength and elastic modulus and will result in decreased strain to failure. While many polymers exhibit these trends, there is evidence that PLA is even more sensitive to strain rate effects compared to other common FDM materials [7] and therefore PLA is a good choice for demonstrating the effect in the current experiment. In one study the authors used only modest variation in crosshead speeds, from 1 to 5 mm/min, and still observed the effects [8]. Other studies used much wider range of speeds, from 0.001 to 100 strain/minute, and demonstrated approximately double the tensile strength and modulus at the higher strain rates [9].

Annealing of printed parts is a possible remedy for some of the problems associated with inter-layer weakness in FDM. Effectiveness of such treatments requires careful selection of both the annealing temperature and the cooling rate after annealing. If done correctly, post-print annealing can change the degree of crystallinity of semi-crystalline polymers, which then can improve mechanical strength and modulus, but with some loss of toughness [10]. Annealing at sufficient temperature followed by rapid cooling may have two-fold effect of 1) reducing internal flaws in essence “healing” some of the inherent voids produced during printing, and 2) promoting more amorphous character in the polymer. If samples are cooled slowly post-annealing the results can be worse than as-printed samples. In the current study, this was a factor in the experiment but was not thoroughly researched to achieve a workable yet beneficial annealing and cooling protocol. The trick is to obtain the desired benefit but without causing undue warping or dimensional changes in the specimens. In Hart’s study, annealing was carried out at 160°C for 2 hours (relative to T_{MP} of 147°C for the polymer) with 10 different cooling rates tested in that study. Cooling rate was a significant factor related to properties of the final samples [10].

Analysis

Materials & Methods

Tensile specimens for this study were made of FDM printed PLA polymer, Overture PLA 3D printer filament on a Prusa™ model MK3™ printer. Printing process parameters were within standard recommended for the material:

Table 1 Material, printer and print parameters used in this study.

Material	Overture® PLA 3D printer filament
Printer	Prusa® MK3
Nozzle Temperature	210°C (215°C for the first layer)
Bed Temperature	60°C
Print Speed	80 mm/sec.
Fill	100%
Samples tested in as-printed condition	For orientation & strain rate
Annealed samples for comparison	Annealed 120°, 2 hours, water quench

Two different part files were used to produce the test specimens. The first part file contained 6 total specimens: two printed lengthwise to the bed, two printed edgewise to the bed, and two printed flat to the bed [Figure 1]. These were used in testing to assess the influence of print orientation on tensile properties. These print pattern (three orientations) was also used in the study of annealing response of 3D printed samples. The second part file contained 6 total specimens with all parts produced flat to the print bed. These flat-printed samples were used to assess the effect of strain rate.

Fig. 1 Two print files for tensile specimens used in this study. Parts marked "x" were printed flat to the printing bed. Up arrow on the other specimens indicates the build direction.

For evaluating print orientation and strain rate, specimens were used in as-printed condition. For the third part of the experiment, samples were annealed prior to testing. The annealing process involved placing samples into an aluminum holding fixture, to prevent warping or dimensional changes of the samples [Figure 2]. The fixture and samples were placed in a lab furnace at 120°C for two hours. The entire fixture with samples was removed and quenched in room temperature water for at least 5 minutes, after which the specimens were removed from the holding fixture.

Tests were run at room temperature. Samples were printed about two weeks prior to testing and stored at room temperature in the lab, with no special pre-conditioning prior to testing.

Dimensions for the test specimens are following ASTM D638, Standard Test Method for Tensile Properties of Plastics for a Type I specimen. There was one minor difference. To accommodate the physical size limitations of the 3D printer

Fig. 2 Holding fixture used to restrain the specimens during annealing and subsequent quenching. There is an aluminum top cover (removed in the photo) to hold the specimens flat and reduce warping.

(specifically, for printing the lengthwise specimens) the overall length of parts was reduced and thus the length of the narrow section of the specimen was also slightly reduced. The narrow test section of the specimens was 50 mm long (versus 57 mm according to the standard), 13 mm wide, by 3.2 mm thick [Figure 3].

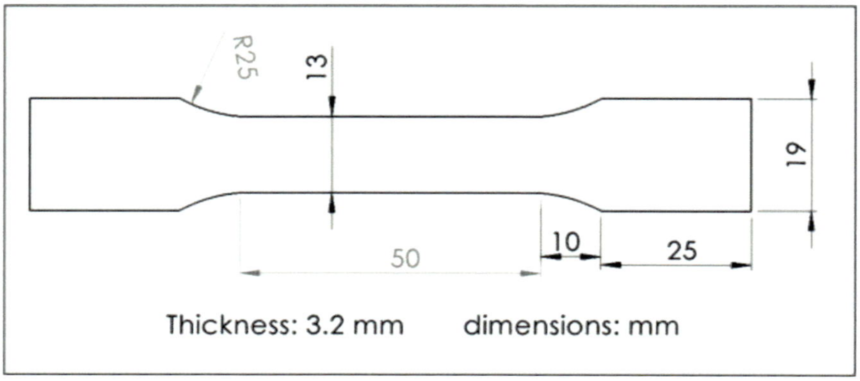

Fig. 3 Nominal dimensions of test specimens are slightly modified from ASTM standard, with reduced length in the middle section. The was done to accommodate printing in the lengthwise orientation in the Prusa printer used.

Method 1 & 3 – Print Orientation & Annealing Response

Tensile testing was done on an Instron 6800-series machine with a model 2580 (50 kN) load cell. Specimens for testing print orientation and annealing response were run at crosshead speed of 0.5 mm/min., for a nominal strain rate of 0.01 mm/mm per minute (1% per minute). This rate is in accordance with the standard, which states "use the lowest speed that produces rupture in 0.5 to 5 minutes." Strains in the experiment were not measured directly using an extensometer, rather they are derived (approximated) in the BlueHill software (Instron) based on crosshead displacement and specimen length in the reduced cross section area. This was done as a compromise which allowed quicker testing and more samples to be completed in limited lab time. All specimens were tested to rupture. Stress and derived strain were recorded as the representative results.

All specimens for annealing and print orientation tests were of parts printed in 3 different orientations in one file, the only difference was in the sample preparation. Testing during lab time was carried out by the instructor, with students observing.

Method 2 – Strain Rate

The only procedural change in the strain-rate method is that crosshead speed was set at three different rates: 0.5 mm/min, 15 mm/min and 500 mm/min (the maximum for the machine). This produced nominal strain rates of 1% per min., 30% per min., and 1000% per minute for the specimens. All specimens for strain-rate testing were from the flat printed parts.

Results

Experiment 1 – Print Orientation

Lengthwise printing clearly underperformed in terms of elongation and strength. This was the expected result. Print layers across the tensile stress area would lead to lower strength and ductility. Test results are shown in Figure 4 and summarized in Table 2. There was only a slight decrease in tensile modulus with print orientation in the lengthwise direction. Between the edgewise and flat printed specimens, edgewise produced the highest strength, while flat-printed produced the highest elongation to failure. In some preliminary testing, the elongation measurement seems to be quite variable, therefore the limited data here does not support a definitive conclusion. One possible explanation would faster cooling of each layer for the edgewise samples. That could potentially change the crystalline/amorphous balance and thus the mechanical properties. This was a repeatable and likely real effect and not just a test anomaly. But more data are needed to make a conclusion.

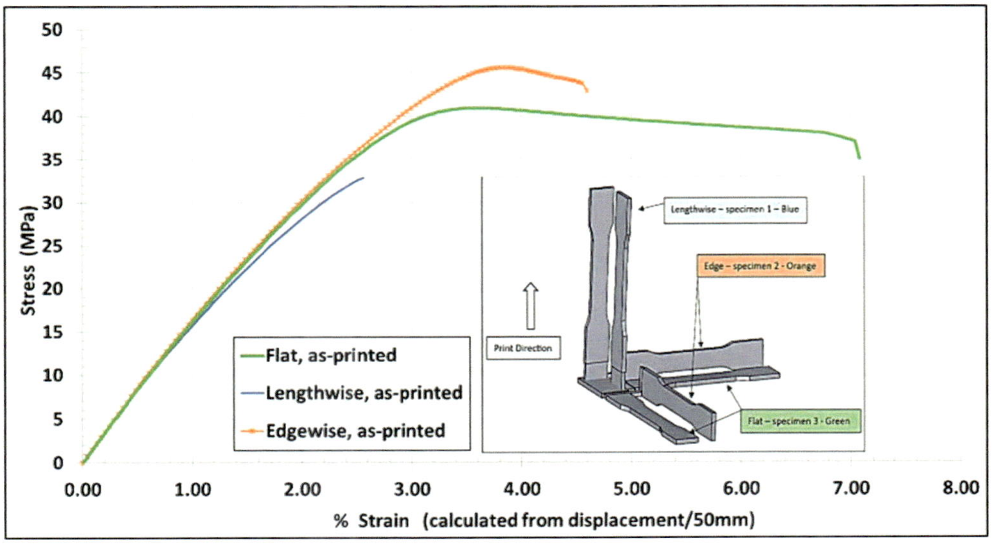

Fig. 4 Stress-strain results comparing the 3 different print orientations.

Table 2 Summary of mechanical properties comparing the 3 different print orientations. Above samples as-printed and tested at 0.5 mm/min (nominal strain rate of 1% per minute).

	Modulus, E [MPa]	Tensile Strength [MPa]	Elongation at Break [%]
Lengthwise	1,570	32.8	2.6
Edgewise	1,640	45.6	4.6
Flat	1,610	41.0	7.1

The test results of this study agree reasonably well but slightly under what the Overture® technical data sheet gives (for comparison, the supplier's values: tensile strength, 47.1 MPa in x-y directions, 38.9.3 MPa in z direction). The ratio of strength in z-direction of 76 to 80% of maximum for the current study, is comparable to the same ratio based on supplier information (83%). Modulus values in the current study are lower compared to published values (Young's modulus, 2641

MPa). Elongation at break was not as high as reported in manufacturer's data (8.2 % in x-y direction, not reported for z-direction). As expected, lengthwise printing gave lower strength and ductility. Mixed results make is difficult to say which is "better" between flat-printed and edgewise. Flat printed had higher elongation but edgewise had higher tensile strength.

Experiment 2 – Strain Rate

Trends shown in the tests on strain rate demonstrate all three expected behaviors. As strain rate increases the ultimate tensile strength increases. As strain rate increases, the elongation to rupture decreases. As strain rate increases, there is a slight increase in the elastic tensile modulus. Test results are shown in Figure 5 and summarized in Table 3.

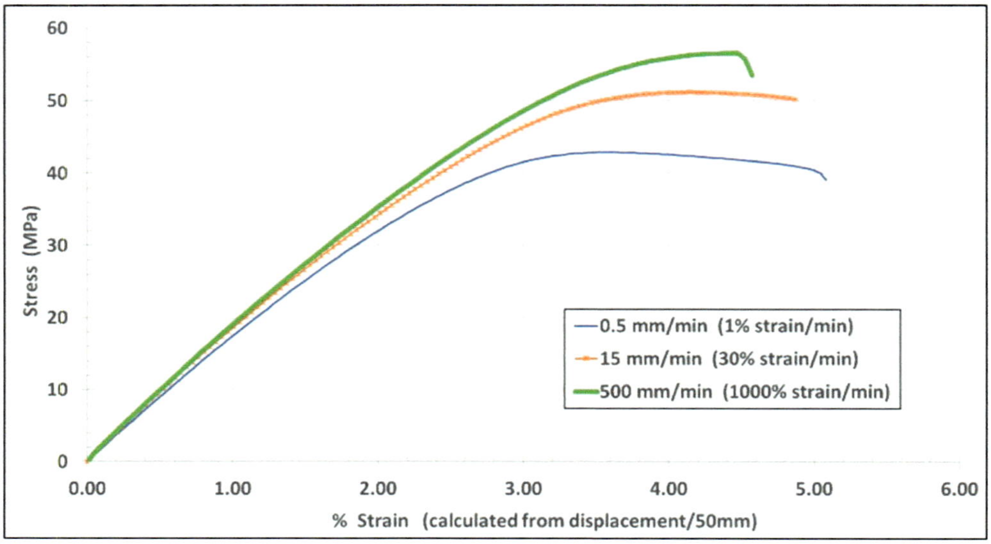

Fig. 5 Stress-strain results comparing strain rates. Flat-printed samples, tested in as-printed condition.

Table 3 Summary of mechanical properties, comparing 3 different strain rates tested.

Crosshead (strain rate)	Modulus, E [MPa]	Tensile Strength [MPa]	Elongation at Break [%]
0.5 mm (1%) /min.	1,750	42.9	5.1
15 mm (30%) /min.	1,870	51.1	4.9
500 mm (1000%) /min.	1,990	56.5	4.8

Experiment 3 – Annealing of FDM Samples, post-printing

Test results for this part of the experiment were counter to what was expected. Most significant was an approximately 30% reduction in elongation at break. It was expected that annealing after printing might improve elongation. Both strength and elastic modulus were improved, but only slightly (2 to 4% increase in strength). Figure 6 shows comparison for two of the annealed samples versus earlier data from the print orientation study.

This part of the experiment was most problematic, both in terms of devising a method for annealing and with generating clear trend in the results. A first attempt at annealing was done without the holding fixture and resulted in severe dimensional changes in the specimens. Using a holding fixture to restrain samples during annealing and cooling helped solve that issue. However, the entire process was quite cumbersome and time consuming.

Annealing response study needs further development to: 1) improve the ease-of-use of the holding fixture and 2) revise the annealing steps to come up with a more favorable response. Ideally, there would be increase in both strength and elongation. Variations in annealing temperature and cooling rate are the key parameters. Both these factors require further study and experimentation.

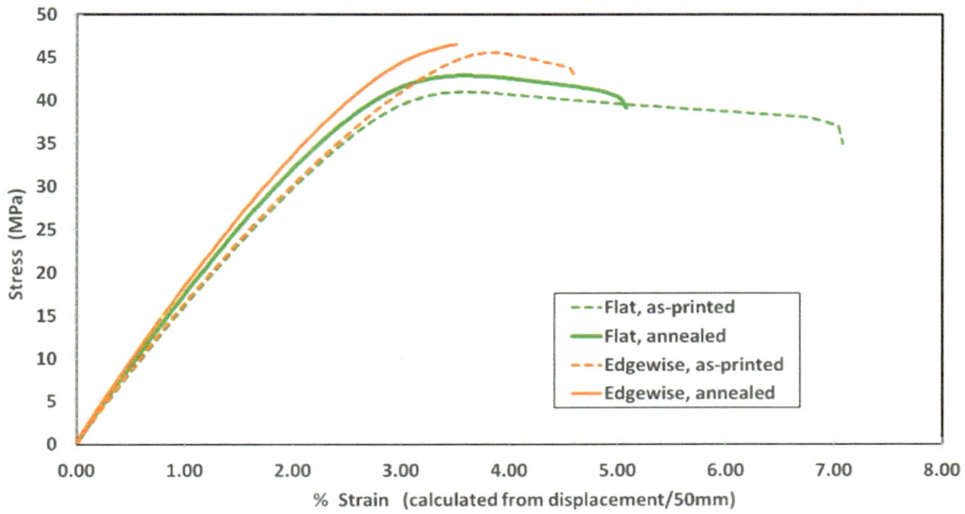

Fig. 6 Comparison of annealed specimens (solid lines) to as-printed specimens (dashed lines).

Table 4 Summary mechanical property comparison for annealed versus as-printed specimens.

	Modulus, E [MPa]	Tensile Strength [MPa]	Elongation at Break [%]
As-printed, Flat	1,610	41.0	7.1
Annealed, Flat	**1,750**	**42.9**	**5.1**
As-printed, Edgewise	1,640	45.6	4.6
Annealed, Edgewise	**1,890**	**46.6**	**3.5**

Conclusions

- Test results for print orientation demonstrated the expected results, were elastic modulus and tensile strength and elongation at failure were measurably lower for lengthwise printed samples.
- Test results for strain-rate also demonstrated that for higher strain rate, 1000% per minute versus 1% per minute, modulus increased by 13% and tensile strength increased by 30%.
- Annealing specimens post-printing proved procedurally difficult to accomplish in a way that both avoided warping and allowed rapid cooling after annealing. Strength was 9-15% higher with annealing, but elongation was about half.
- From the viewpoint of using this as an educational experience, the lab is a successful one. It clearly demonstrates differences in mechanical behavior of polymers versus metals. Additional concepts relating to prior courses can be effectively reviewed, and some new concepts relating to manufacturing processes are introduced.

Acknowledgments Thanks to Justin Summer at MSOE for his help with making all the samples for this study and thanks to Kevin Hart for his assistance with the planning.

References

1. Kattan, C., Grossnickle Peterson, E., & Miller, K. "Revising Teacher Candidates Beliefs and Knowledge of the Leaning Styles Neuromyth" Contemporary Educational Psychology, 77, 102269. June 2024.
2. Kirscher, P.A. "Stop Propagating the Learning Styles Myth" Computers & Education 106, 166-171. 2017.
3. MatWeb, (n.d.-a.) "Online materials information resource" http://MatWeb.com/ 2025.
4. ASTM, "D638-14 Standard Test Method for Tensile Properties of Plastics" ASTM International, 2014.
5. Overture, Technical Data Sheet: PLA v5.1, Overture 3D, Aug. 2024.
6. Polymaker, Technical Data Sheet: PolyLite™ PLA v5.3, Polymaker US, 2024.
7. Vidakis, N., Petousis, M, et al. "On the Strain Rate Sensitivity of Fused Filament Fabrication (FFF) Processed PLA, ABS, PETG, PA6, and PP Thermoplastic Polymers" Polymers 12(12) 2924, 2020.

8. Balasubramanian, M., Saravanan, R., Shanmugam, V. "Impact of strain rate on mechanical properties of polylactic acid fabricated by fusion deposition modeling" Polymers for Advanced Technologies, Mar. 2024.
9. Luo, J., Luo, Q., Zhang, G., Li, Q., Sun, G. "On strain rate and temperature dependent mechanical properties and constitutive models for additively manufactured polylactic acid (PLA) materials" Thin-Walled Structures 179, 109624, 2022.
10. Hart, K., Dunn, R., Wetzel, E. "Increased facture toughness of additively manufactured semi-crystalline thermoplastics via thermal annealing" Polymer, 211, 123091, 2020.

For Product Safety Concerns and Information please contact our
EU representative GPSR@taylorandfrancis.com Taylor & Francis
Verlag GmbH, Kaufingerstraße 24, 80331 München, Germany